Praise for *Endless Customers*

"From the first moment I heard Marcus speak about the principles of *Endless Customers*, I knew it was exactly what we needed to take each one of our different businesses in Mazzella Companies to the next level. And although I knew it would work, I never imagined this system would have such a profound influence on how well we've become known in our industry. Today, Mazzella is the leading voice in each of our spaces, driving incredible awareness, leads, and business. *Everyone* knows who we are. As a fellow business owner, I can tell you this system works. Follow it."

—Tony Mazzella, CEO, Mazzella Companies

"In 2021, after 30-plus years of operating in a very specific way, we made a bold shift away from high-pressure sales tactics and gimmicky marketing offers. I was initially fearful of the potential negative impact on our leads and sales, but the Endless Customers System provided a clear and actionable roadmap for this transition. Since then, we've experienced a significant increase in qualified leads and higher close rates, proving that trust-based marketing truly works."

—Ryan Shutt, CEO, Southwest Exteriors

"Marcus Sheridan is not only a home run keynote speaker at my events but also a valuable contributor to three of my books. His insights consistently deliver practical, actionable, and transformative strategies. *Endless Customers* is yet another testament to his ability to steer businesses toward long-lasting success."

—Joe Pulizzi, bestselling author of
Content Inc.* and *Epic Content Marketing

"I've long been a superfan of the forward-thinking principles Marcus preaches. Now he's evolved their perspective into this comprehensive, easy-to-follow system. The best kind of content builds trust first, then drives results. *Endless Customers* shows you how."

—Ann Handley, Chief Content Officer,
MarketingProfs and WSJ bestselling
author of *Everybody Writes*

"*Endless Customers* delivers far more than marketing advice—it's a blueprint for business transformation. At Applied Educational Systems, implementing these principles revolutionized how we earned customer trust and delivered value. The results spoke volumes: we went from virtually no organic leads to generating 30,000 leads annually in our niche market, generated $27 million in revenue directly from our content, grew revenue 5.5 times, and earned five consecutive spots on the Inc. 5000 list. This book isn't theory—it's a proven path to sustainable growth, even in specialized markets.

—**Jim Schultz, former CEO, Applied Education Systems, and Vistage Chair**

"Before implementing the principles of *Endless Customers*, our digital presence just wasn't cutting it. Our website was filled with fluffy content written by various freelancers, and it didn't fulfill our buyers' needs. Today, we're bringing in more than $270k per month from organic leads and have seen a $1 million increase in revenue."

—**Dave Owens, Director of Marketing and Sales Management, RoofCrafters**

"As someone who has lived and breathed the principles of *Endless Customers*, I can attest to its transformative power. I was able to build unprecedented authority in my industry, increasing leads by 2,942% and doubling our business. In fact, the success was so profound that we were able to acquire an entire franchise, expanding our reach and impact beyond what I ever imagined. Additionally, the Endless Customers movement has profoundly impacted our company culture by getting the entire team aligned and working toward the same goal, fostering a sense of shared purpose and collaboration."

—**Mark Massey, Owner, RetroFoam of Michigan**

"*Endless Customers* isn't just a book—it's a career-defining playbook. As someone who's grown from marketing manager to CMO, I can attest that the principles in this book have been instrumental in my professional journey. I've had the privilege of implementing the Endless Customers System at two different companies, and both are still fully embracing these principles today because of the results they continue to see."

—**Kendall Guinn, CMO, LV Collective**

"*Endless Customers* is the definitive guide for how you can meet more of your perfect customers earlier, earn their trust and help them repeatedly choose you over your competition. If you lead a business and have not yet embraced the core lessons in this book, then you are about to be really mad at yourself for not getting started earlier. It's the honest cheat code for new client acquisition."

—Phil M. Jones, Creator of Exactly What to Say

"The principles put forth in *Endless Customers* and *They Ask, You Answer* provided us with a formulaic approach to content marketing success. It helped us prioritize and execute a written and video-centric marketing strategy that enhanced our SEO efforts and increased monthly website visitors nearly 500% in the first 12 months. This traffic continues to be a significant source of leads and revenue for our business."

—Dan Godla, Founder and CEO, ThoroughCare

"*Endless Customers* laid the foundation to transform our small local roofing company into the leading source of roofing information across the United States. This book will completely change how you approach marketing and selling in ways guaranteed to make you stand out from the competition. After five years of following the system, I can honestly say it's been one of our better investments!"

—Bill Ragan, President, Bill Ragan Roofing

"Smart marketing is about help, not hype. *Endless Customers* gives you the roadmap to create content that solves problems, builds trust, and wins revenue. Recommended!"

—Jay Baer, author of *The Time to Win: How to Exceed Customers' Need for Speed*

"Implementing the Endless Customers System has been transformative for our company. Not only has it empowered our leaders to develop new skills, but it has also fostered a culture of growth and collaboration throughout the entire organization. We've made a significant shift toward a more client-centric approach by focusing on education and transparency. As a result, we're building stronger relationships with our clients and seeing incredible ROI. *Endless Customers* has been a game-changer for Custom Built."

—Michael Flory, Owner, CEO, and
Visionary, Custom Built

"For years, we struggled with how to stand out in an HVAC industry that was jam-packed with competition. Fast forward to now, *Endless Customers* has changed how we do business. Our competition doesn't like it. We're raising the standard 10-fold in the industry. Since going all-in on *Endless Customers*, Fire & Ice can trace more than $1 million in revenue directly to organic sources."

—Scott Merritt, Owner, Fire &
Ice Heating and Air Conditioning

"Marcus knocked it out of the park! He's enhanced the *They Ask, You Answer* methodology and provided all of us with a clear roadmap to *Endless Customers*. I'm also using this book to train my AI tools to elevate our standards in content, video, and sales effectiveness."

—Keven Ellison, VP of Marketing, AIS

ENDLESS CUSTOMERS

THEY ASK, YOU ANSWER 3.0

ENDLESS CUSTOMERS

A PROVEN SYSTEM TO BUILD TRUST, DRIVE SALES, AND BECOME THE MARKET LEADER

MARCUS **SHERIDAN**

AND THE TEAM AT **IMPACT**

WILEY

Published by John Wiley & Sons, Inc., Hoboken, New Jersey.
Published simultaneously in Canada.

For general information on our other products and services or for technical support, please contact our Customer Care Department within the United States at (800) 762-2974, outside the United States at (317) 572-3993 or fax (317) 572-4002.

Wiley also publishes its books in a variety of electronic formats. Some content that appears in print may not be available in electronic formats. For more information about Wiley products, visit our web site at www.wiley.com.

Library of Congress Cataloging-in-Publication Data is Available:

ISBN: 978-1-394-28278-4 (cloth)
ISBN: 978-1-394-28279-1 (ePub)
ISBN: 978-1-394-28280-7 (ePDF)

Cover Design: Joe Rinaldi
Author Photo: Courtesy of the Author
SKY10098776_022425

*This book is for the disruptors—the ones
who dare to reimagine their industries,
challenge convention, and lead with honesty
and boldness, proving that mediocrity
is never the only option.*

Contents

SECTION 7   Putting It All Together   189

Preface:

Endless Customers: Evolving Beyond *They Ask, You Answer*

The world changed forever on November 30, 2022.

That was the day when millions of people first experienced ChatGPT and suddenly realized that everything we thought we knew about information, search, and the internet was about to be transformed. In that moment, I knew that my previous book, *They Ask, You Answer*, needed to evolve into something bigger—much bigger.

Back in 2017, when I first published *They Ask, You Answer*, I shared what seemed like an impossible story: how my swimming pool company went from the brink of bankruptcy during the 2008 crash to becoming the most visited pool website in the world. Eventually, we even expanded into manufacturing with dealers across the nation. The book's message—a radical commitment to answering (online) every single customer question with unprecedented honesty—resonated far beyond what I could have imagined, touching more than 100,000 businesses worldwide.

But that was just the beginning.

What we're experiencing now isn't just another technological shift—it's a fundamental reimagining of how humans interact with information. Every business owner and leader must ask themselves, "If we live in a world where artificial intelligence (AI) can instantly generate answers to any question, what does it truly mean to be trusted? How do we stand out when everyone has access to the same tools and information?" The answers to these questions aren't just important—they're existential to your business.

Endless Customers isn't just an evolution of *They Ask, You Answer*—it's a complete reimagining of what it means to build trust and attract customers in the AI era. While the core philosophy remains the same—an obsession with understanding and serving your buyer—the methods, strategies, and thinking must be exponentially more ambitious.

This book introduces a proven system that transcends platforms, technologies, and trends. It's not about adapting to ChatGPT or whatever comes next—it's about positioning your business to thrive in any future, using principles that will remain relevant regardless of how dramatically the landscape changes.

Our team at IMPACT has seen these principles work wonders for our diverse group of clients worldwide, and they can work for you, too.

The businesses that will dominate the next decade won't be the ones with the best AI tools or the biggest marketing budgets. They'll be the ones who dare to think differently about trust, transparency, and customer relationships. They'll be the ones willing to do what their competitors won't even consider. They'll be the ones who understand that in a world of infinite information, **trust becomes the ultimate currency**.

The path to becoming one of these businesses isn't easy. It requires more than simply answering customer questions—it demands a fundamental shift in how you think about your relationship with your market. But for those willing to embrace this change, the reward is nothing less than what the title promises: *Endless Customers*.

You're opening this book because you sense that the old ways of doing business are fading. You're right. The principles in these pages will show you how to build a business that doesn't just adapt to the AI revolution but leads it—a business that becomes so trusted, so essential to its customers, that growth becomes inevitable. And ultimately, it becomes a business that transforms into the most known and trusted voice in its market.

The future belongs to those who are brave enough to reimagine what's possible. It is my great hope you will join them.

Introduction

Steve Sheinkopf was in trouble.

The kitchen appliance industry was going through a major shakeup, and retailers were struggling to stay afloat. His company, Yale Appliance, a family-owned retailer based in Boston, was no exception. For nearly a century, Yale Appliance had served its community. But between the explosion of ecommerce, big-box stores squeezing margins, and constant supply chain issues, it was hard for Steve to make the headway he wanted with his business.

He had been trying to get traction with online content and other marketing efforts, but what he was doing was falling flat. Nothing seemed to be working. Having dedicated his career to growing the family business, Steve worried that if he didn't crack this code, he would face the same fate as so many of his competitors who were downsizing or closing up shop.

That's when Steve came across the concepts in my previous book, *They Ask, You Answer*. Intrigued, he reached out, and before long we were on the phone discussing his business. He wanted to understand why his efforts weren't gaining more traction online. After a short conversation, the reason became incredibly clear. "If you want more customers, you need to stop doing what every other appliance retailer is doing," I told him. "Start giving your buyers what they want—not what you want, but what *they* need to feel confident and informed."

I explained further. "That means obsessing over their questions, fears, worries, and concerns. Answer every single question honestly and transparently, right there on your website, for everyone to see."

Then I pushed him to think bigger. "Tackle topics your competitors are afraid to touch. Break the unwritten rules of your industry. When you focus solely on empowering your buyers with the information and experience they crave, something incredible will happen: You'll earn their trust. And when you earn their trust, you earn their business. Do this consistently, and you'll capture the market's attention, transform your company, and see numbers you never imagined."

Many CEOs have reached out over the years, but none have taken action like Steve. At the time, I had no idea how seriously he would take my advice. But it sparked a transformation that still stuns me almost a decade later.

Steve set out on a relentless mission to become the most known and trusted brand in the entire home appliance space. He wanted anyone in the market for a new appliance to find him, learn from him, and ultimately trust him enough to make a purchase.

First, Steve declared his mission to his company. He even went as far as mandating that if you work for Yale Appliance, you have a responsibility to help create content. He knew his sales team fielded hundreds of questions daily, and he knew they had the answers that helped his customers buy.

Next, Steve realized that for this mission to succeed, he had to stop viewing his business as just an appliance store. Instead, he had to see it as a "media company" leading the way in buyer education for all things home appliances. He also understood that this effort couldn't simply be outsourced to an agency—it had to come from within his organization, with the expertise and perspectives coming directly from him and his team. So he invested in the right internal resources to make it happen.

After that, he worked closely with his team to brainstorm all the questions customers had asked them, creating a content calendar that would last well over a year. Then, they got to work. They started answering every single one of those questions thoroughly and publishing at least three new articles a week, all while continually adding new content ideas to the backlog.

Steve left no stone unturned when it came to answering questions. He shared what people were saying about products after they'd bought them, compared options with honest pros and cons, and openly discussed pricing, warranties, and whether products were worth the investment based on specific needs.

Recognizing the power of video, Steve expanded to YouTube and social media. He understood that video did more than answer questions—it built human connections and revealed things never seen before in his industry.

After a few years, Steve had published hundreds of articles and videos. But one of his gutsiest moves came when he decided to answer a question every buyer had: *Which appliance brands are serviced the least?*

Think about it. When people buy a new appliance, they're often replacing one they're tired of repairing. Steve had access to data from 40,000 service calls each year and knew exactly which brands held up best—and which didn't.

But he also understood the risks. Publishing this information could upset major brands like Wolf, GE, and Bosch, potentially straining critical vendor relationships.

Should he take the chance?

Ultimately, Steve remembered his guiding philosophy: If he wanted to earn his market's trust, his priority had to be giving buyers what they wanted to know.

So he did something that sent shockwaves through the appliance industry. He published an article on his website revealing the number of units sold for each brand the previous year, along with the number of service calls required for each. Reading this article, you'd learn not only which brand was the least serviced (congratulations, Gaggenau!) but also which brand topped the list for service calls. (I'll let you Google that one.)

Gutsy? Yes.

Courageous? Absolutely.

Worth it? Without a doubt.

The article has been read more than *one million times* on the Yale Appliance website. It has generated hundreds of thousands of dollars in sales revenue—not to mention the immense trust and brand awareness it created for his business.

Its success was undeniable. Steve now produces a yearly article and video series on this topic, transparently sharing the previous year's data and letting the facts speak for themselves. A decade into living the principles of *They Ask, You Answer* (now *Endless Customers*), Steve continues to evolve, constantly pushing the boundaries of what's possible in sales and marketing.

Before implementing these principles, Yale Appliance was a $37 million company with one store. Since then, it has grown into a $100-million-plus operation with four stores, thriving through a pandemic and increasing margins year after year in an ever-more competitive industry.

Extraordinary, isn't it?

Steve and Yale have become one of the most known and trusted brands in the appliance industry—all because he had the courage to do what no one else in his space was willing to do, even though buyers were clearly asking for it.

Well done, Steve. You are, without question, the ultimate industry disruptor.

Steve's story is a testament to what's possible when you focus on empowering your customers. And it's a challenge—to every business leader, every brand, and every marketing and sales team:

Be bolder.

Be braver.

Be more disruptive.

And always be willing to give buyers what they need.

A Note from the Author

Thank you for picking up a copy of Endless Customers. *If you're reading this and feel inspired, or if you have questions about how to implement these ideas in your business, don't hesitate to reach out. I'd love to hear from you.*

You can contact me directly at Marcus@EndlessCustomers.com. I'll do my best to respond personally and quickly. I look forward to hearing from you!

SECTION

1 | Preview of the Endless Customers System™

Customer acquisition today isn't simply about having a great product or service. Buyers are more informed, more skeptical, and more impatient than ever—while attention spans are shorter, competition is fiercer, and trust in brands is at an all-time low. On top of that, search engines and social media platforms now excel at keeping users on their sites, creating a "zero-click" environment that can starve you of traffic and leads.

But here's the good news: These challenges also present a massive opportunity.

In this section, we'll explore why businesses are seeing stalled deals, shrinking website traffic, ineffectual outsourcing, and increasingly elusive brand recognition—and, more importantly, how to turn the tide in your favor. You'll learn:

- How shifts in buyer behavior have transformed the sales process into a self-service, "touchless" journey.
- Why the competition for trust is the real battle—and how to win it.
- Why Google's evolution toward zero-click search is forcing brands to rethink the way they reach and engage prospects.

1

■ How you can stand out in an oversaturated market by empowering your buyers, embracing transparency, and demonstrating credibility at every touchpoint.

Whether you're struggling to grow your business or determined to maintain your lead, this section sets the stage for the frameworks, strategies, and mindset shifts you'll discover in *Endless Customers*—a proven roadmap to creating a brand so known and trusted that new business flows naturally to you.

So buckle up.

It's time to reimagine what real customer acquisition looks like in the modern age.

1

Why Customer Acquisition Is Harder Than Ever— And How to Fix It

Acquiring new customers is tougher than ever.

If you're like most business leaders, you might be asking yourself, "Why is it so hard? We've poured our hearts and souls into building this company. We've got a product or service that's better than our competitors. We've set up systems, refined our processes, and consistently deliver on our promises to customers. So why is it so difficult to bring in new business and grow?"

Or maybe you're on the other side of the fence. Your business is doing well, maybe you're even outperforming your competitors right now. You've built something solid, and you're seeing results. But you know you can be doing even better. You know the market changes fast, and you're thinking, "What do we need to do to protect our position to stay ahead?"

If either of these sounds familiar, you're not alone. Whether you're struggling to grow or want to protect your current success, many businesses are facing similar challenges when it comes to customer acquisition.

Chances are, you're experiencing one or more of the following frustrations:

- **Stalled deals.** The deals sitting in your pipeline take longer and longer to close—if they close at all. It feels like every decision is drawn out, and you're left wondering if you'll ever get a commitment.
- **Declining website traffic and lead generation.** You used to generate consistent traffic from search engines, driving qualified leads into your funnel. But that traffic has slowed down. Leads aren't flowing in like they used to, and the ones that do trickle in aren't as qualified.
- **Losing to competitors.** Even though your product or service is superior, you're watching potential customers choose the competition—often without even speaking to your team. It stings when you know your company offers something better, yet you can't seem to get that message across.
- **Ineffective outsourcing.** You've hired an agency to run your marketing, investing significant resources into the partnership. The results, however, are underwhelming. The leads you were promised simply aren't there, and the return on investment (ROI) is nowhere near what you expected.
- **You're not a "known and trusted" brand.** Sure, you've been in business for a while, but for some reason your brand in the market just isn't standing out. You can't seem to grab the world's attention, despite your best efforts.

These frustrations are widespread in the business world, and there are clear reasons why so many companies are feeling stuck.

Why Are You Experiencing These Frustrations?

First, there's a massive trust deficit.

Consumers have been burned too many times. Whether it's false advertising, under-delivered promises, or bad customer experiences, trust in brands is at an all-time low.[1] People are afraid of making a mistake, so they're more cautious and skeptical than ever. They're questioning everything before they buy.

Can you relate?

If you're like most people, you've likely experienced this in your own life. For this reason, it's not just about having a great product anymore; it's about earning trust—and lots of it. If buyers don't trust that you'll deliver on what you've promised them, it doesn't matter how good your product is—they won't buy.

Second, search engines and social media have changed the game.

For more than 20 years, you could count on Google to drive traffic to your website. People searched, they clicked on the results, and if you were ranking well, you got traffic.

Not anymore.

Today's search engines are packed with distractions: ads disguised as organic results, featured snippets, and AI-generated overviews that keep users on the results page instead of driving them to your website. The consequence? Organic traffic, once a reliable source of growth for many businesses, is rapidly drying up. And as AI evolves, the shift toward a "zero-click" search experience is accelerating, delivering users exactly what they need without ever leaving the search results page.

This means you can no longer build your house solely on Google.

And it's the same with social media. Today, when you create a post that includes an external link, it simply won't reach as many people. These platforms are only interested in one thing—holding visitors as long as possible to boost ad revenue—and the longer people stay, the more ads they see.

Third, buyers are more informed than ever and demand answers.

The way people buy has fundamentally shifted. Research shows that, on average, 80% of the buying process, whether it is business to business (B2B) or business to consumer (B2C), is completed *before* a prospect even talks to a salesperson—and that percentage keeps climbing.[2] During this time, buyers are diligently gathering information by researching, comparing options, reading reviews, and narrowing down their choices.

Essentially, buyers today are *info-vores*—and they expect to be fed the information they're craving.

Fourth, buyers want control and the option for self-service.

They're looking for a buying process that requires minimal interaction with a salesperson—what we call a "touchless buying experience." This means they prefer to research, compare, and even make purchasing decisions on their own terms, only engaging with sales when they're fully ready and comfortable. They won't wait for a response, they refuse to jump through hoops, and they expect the process to be easy and frictionless. And when they do reach out, they expect a seamless transition from their independent research to a productive sales conversation.

If your team isn't ready to meet your buyers where they are—by giving them what they want, when they want it, and how they want it—you risk losing them. And once they're gone, they're not coming back.

Fifth, the competition (and noise) is fierce.

There's more content being produced now than ever before. Every brand, big or small, is vying for attention. The noise is deafening. And when you combine that with impatient attention spans and content fatigue, it becomes harder to break through. People are tuning out quickly, and if you don't capture their attention in those first few seconds, they're gone.

Sixth, the post-pandemic world brings new challenges.

Companies are facing rapid market swings, with one quarter bringing a surge of new business, and the next, crickets. For many, it's a rollercoaster of unpredictability. B2B companies especially are seeing tighter budgets and prolonged decision-making cycles. This stop-and-go rhythm is making it harder than ever to plan, forecast, or grow with any consistency.

Finally, most content (and marketing in general) is unoriginal, boring, and lacks soul.

This is a hard truth for many businesses to accept. The majority of company-generated content being created today simply isn't very effective. It doesn't truly answer the *real* questions buyers have about your products or services. Instead, it's generic, bland, and often too self-serving.

This criticism extends beyond content and applies to much of the corporate marketing that exists in the world today. If we're being honest, most marketing campaigns are incredibly boring, stale, and entirely risk-averse.

If followed correctly, the Endless Customers System™ is the antithesis of this "lowering of the bar" that plagues so many businesses and marketing departments today. In contrast, it pushes brands to raise the bar and dare to be different, putting the customer, honesty, and transparency at the center of everything you put out into the world.

A Shift in Mindset

When you put all of these factors together, it's no wonder why businesses are struggling. There's a disconnect between what businesses think buyers need and what buyers are *actually* looking for.

The good news? It doesn't have to be this way.

Yes, the landscape has changed, but that also means there's a huge opportunity for those willing to adjust, adapt, and do things differently.

Your business can stand out.

You can market better and build trust.

You can create content that resonates with prospects, addresses their real concerns, and moves them through the buying process without all the friction they're currently experiencing.

You can do all of this and experience continual success.

But this requires a shift in mindset.

Companies can't keep doing what worked five or even two years ago. Buyers are smarter, more informed, and more skeptical than ever. They expect authenticity, speed, and a seamless, hassle-free experience. The brands that will succeed in the future are the ones that embrace these changes head-on.

To successfully implement the principles of this book, the mindset of your company (especially your leadership team) must be as follows:

- Buyers are more informed, demanding, and impatient than they've ever been, and they're not going back.
- Our company must evolve to meet these buyers where they are or risk being left behind.
- We must do what it takes to become the most known and trusted brand in our space.
- We need to be willing to do things no one else in our industry is doing and become true disruptors in our space.
- To achieve all these things, we must think and operate like a "media company."

This book will give you two foundational frameworks (as well as a series of supporting tools):

1. **The 4 Pillars of a Known and Trusted Brand.** This is a guiding series of statements your business must adopt in order to reframe your mindset.
2. **The 5 Components of Endless Customers.** These form a clear roadmap to turn this mindset into proven actions that will build a

trusted, recognized brand and generate an endless flow of new business and customers.

Let's quickly introduce you to both of these elements.

Preview: The 4 Pillars of a Known and Trusted Brand

The heart of the Endless Customers System isn't about shouting louder or chasing every lead that comes your way. Instead, it's about building a brand so trustworthy, so recognizable, that when buyers have a problem to solve, they think of you first—every single time.

As we move through this book, we'll explore **The 4 Pillars of a Known and Trusted Brand**, which is the foundation of *Endless Customers*, all working together to earn trust and position your company as the go-to leader in your market.

Here are the four pillars:

1. **Say** what others in your space aren't willing to say.
2. **Show** what others in your space aren't willing to show.
3. **Sell** in a way others in your space aren't willing to sell.
4. **Be more human** than others in your space are willing to be.

On the surface, these pillars probably look like simple, common sense. And the truth is—they are.

But can you honestly say that your company or organization is *consistently* doing all four of these things better than 95% of your competitors? I've posed this question to thousands of audiences, clients, and community members around the world, and fewer than 1% of them can confidently say they are.

The beauty of Endless Customers System lies in its simplicity. Anyone can understand it, apply it, and achieve extraordinary results with it. We've seen it work countless times across industries, sectors, and niches—globally and at every stage of business growth.

Why is this? Well, because if you take these four pillars and apply each of them to your business's sales and marketing activities, they boil down into five simple components you need to get right.

Preview: The 5 Components of Endless Customers

To successfully build The 4 Pillars of a Known and Trusted Brand at your organization, you'll need to master **The 5 Components of Endless Customers**. These are the five elements of your business that must be in place and optimized to reach the milestones we've found lead to sustainable success.

We'll explain each of the components and what success with them looks like in the final section of the book, "Putting It All Together." But as you can imagine, the guidance is quite simple—finding the right mix of activities that lead your business to becoming a known and trusted brand, which generates more and better leads, and ultimately results in endless customers.

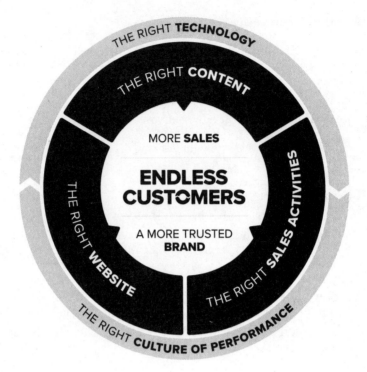

The five components are:

1. The Right Content
2. The Right Website
3. The Right Sales Activities
4. The Right Technology
5. The Right Culture of Performance

When these components are dialed in, you're much more likely to achieve sustainable success. Miss just one, though, and you'll feel it—a gap in performance, a crack in the foundation, or a missed opportunity.

Yet, even as simple as these concepts sound, the sad reality is that most companies (despite knowing in their gut they should be doing this) won't take action—or won't execute it well.

Why is that? The reasons vary, and we'll explore them throughout this book.

But before we move forward, let's take a moment to be candid about who the Endless Customers approach *is* for and who it *isn't* for.

Is Endless Customers Right for You?

It's important to be upfront about who will, and who will not, benefit most from the Endless Customers System.

Generally speaking, Endless Customers is best suited for companies with annual revenues between $1 million and $100 million. Why? Because companies in this range are often capable of bringing their marketing in-house and are nimble enough to implement real cultural change. They're also willing and able to push boundaries, break industry norms, and do what's never been done before in their space, especially when it comes to the way they sell and market their products or services.

This doesn't mean, however, that businesses outside of this range can't benefit from Endless Customers also. We've seen companies both larger and smaller than this find success with this system if they're committed to making it work.

Endless Customers is for you and your business if:

- You aspire to make your company the most known and trusted brand in your market—whether you operate locally, regionally, nationally, or globally.
- You're ready to build a foundation for long-term growth and establish yourself as the "known" leader in your space.
- You want to take control of your customer acquisition process and success, instead of relying on outside agencies.
- You look at your industry and feel deeply that you could improve it by raising standards of excellence across the board while becoming more obsessed with what customers truly need and deserve.
- You're tired of the boring, soulless status quo in your industry (sales, marketing, and customer service) and are ready to shake things up.

We've also seen many companies that run on EOS® (Entrepreneurial Operating System) or participate in programs like Vistage, EO (Entrepreneurs' Organization), or YPO (Young Presidents' Organization) thrive with the principles of Endless Customers. Why? Because these organizations share a focus on learning, continuous improvement, and strong systems—values that align perfectly with the approach outlined in this book.

That said, Endless Customers isn't for everyone. **If you're looking for a quick fix, this system might not be right for you.**

The journey to Endless Customers requires a long-term commitment from leadership and a willingness to challenge the status quo. If you're not ready to invest the time and effort—or if your organization isn't prepared to disrupt—then this might not be the path for you.

Where Endless Customers Works Best

The Endless Customers System is most effective for businesses where buyers tend to do significant research and engage deeply with content before making a purchase. We've seen incredible success in industries like B2B services, professional services, construction, healthcare, home improvement, insurance, manufacturing, home goods, and real estate, among others. These are sectors where trust is paramount, and buyers are looking for expertise before they make a decision.

On the flipside, if you're in an industry with short sales cycles—where buyers don't engage with educational content and instead make quick, impulse decisions—this approach may not be as effective. For example, if you run a restaurant or a convenience store, Endless Customers might not be your best option. However, even in these types of businesses, certain elements of Endless Customers can still be adapted and applied depending on your specific context and goals.

The Journey Ahead

By the time you finish this book, you'll have a roadmap to transform your business into the most known and trusted brand in your space. This earned trust will then give you the ability to generate more qualified leads, close deals faster, and ultimately, grow your business—potentially to heights you never dreamt possible.

And remember, this isn't just a theory—it's practical, actionable advice based on proven strategies that have worked for companies of all shapes and sizes all over the world. If you're ready to embrace change, challenge the status quo, and become the leader in your market, this book is for you.

Welcome to *Endless Customers*.

Let's get started.

Access the Endless Customers Companion Guide

We've created the Endless Customers (EC) Companion Guide to enhance your experience with this book. Since AI and emerging technologies are rapidly reshaping sales and marketing, the guide allows us to keep everything up to date and provide hands-on tools as you read.

Here's what you'll find inside the EC Companion Guide:

- Access to the Endless Customers tools mentioned in the book.
- A growing library of real-world success stories and case studies.
- Expanded marketing and sales recommendations to build on the book's strategies.
- Software suggestions to support your Endless Customers journey.
- Recommended AI prompts to help you succeed.
- A bonus chapter: "From Endless Customers to Endless Job Candidates".

Now is a great time to access the guide. Just scan the QR code, and you'll have everything you need right at your fingertips.

2

The 4 Pillars of a Known and Trusted Brand

There are two types of mindsets most people will have when reading this book.

The first type of mindset is one that says, "Yes, we could do that," or "This is so obvious, why aren't we doing it already?" That person will thrive with the Endless Customers System™.

The second type, however, will read this and—when challenged to think *very* differently about sales and marketing—will default to saying something like, "Yeah, well, this system may have worked for others, but we're different."

Ah, yes—"But we're different." This mindset poisons the waters of business innovation.

"That wouldn't work for our buyer."
"We can't do that in a regulated industry."
"Our products are too complex for this."
"That's just not how it works in our space."

You might have already found yourself thinking along these lines in the first few pages of this book. It's an easy trap to fall into. As humans, we resist change. We also tend to "defend" the way we've always done things because admitting otherwise can feel like admitting we've been wrong.

But if you're going to get anything from this book, you have to overcome that resistance right now. Here's how—boil down every recommendation in *Endless Customers* to one single question: **Will this induce more trust?**

That's it. *That's* the question.

As you move through the book, when you're tempted to say, "This won't work for us," stop and ask yourself, "But if we did this, would it induce more trust?" If the answer is yes, then everything else will fall into place. Why? **Because the *one thing* all businesses have in common is that we're all in a battle for winning trust—every single day.** And as long as businesses exist, that won't change.

Technology will change.

Platforms like Google, Facebook, and ChatGPT will change.

But the need to build trust will not.

That's because trust is a principle. And principles don't come and go.

This is why it doesn't matter whether you're B2C or B2B, local or national, big or small, product or service—Endless Customers works because its entire aim is to help you become more known and drive more trust.

I know we're making a big deal about trust, but unless you truly understand and deeply believe in the fundamental importance of driving trust in your business, you won't experience any breakthroughs from this book—and you certainly won't unlock the extraordinary sales and marketing innovations that will inevitably follow.

So open your heart and mind, and watch the ideas that follow.

Ostrich Marketing: The Enemy of Trust

Now that we've established trust as the centerpiece of your business and brand, and that it will remain so for years to come, let's revisit Chapter 1. There, we learned that The 4 Pillars of a Known and Trusted Brand are:

1. **Say** what others in your space aren't willing to say.
2. **Show** what others in your space aren't willing to show.
3. **Sell** in a way others in your space aren't willing to sell.
4. **Be more human** than others in your space are willing to be.

As buyers, we want this from companies we're considering buying from, and it forms the foundation of all our purchasing decisions. Yet these are the very things companies shy away from.

Most companies and brands aren't willing to do any of the four. They aren't willing to say what buyers want to hear. They aren't willing to show what buyers want to see. They aren't willing to sell in a way buyers want to be sold to. And they aren't willing to put themselves out there and humanize their brand in the ways buyers prefer.

We call this phenomenon **Ostrich Marketing.**

As the myth goes, when an ostrich encounters a problem, it buries its head in the sand. Much like the ostrich, businesses often do the same in their approach to sales and marketing. Instead of addressing the toughest questions buyers want answered online, they ignore them. Instead of selling the way buyers prefer, businesses often force their buyers into frustrating "sales processes."

There are countless examples of this (which we'll explore throughout this book), but the fact remains that you cannot become the most known and trusted brand in your market if you ignore the questions, fears, and needs of your buyers. The two simply cannot co-exist.

We must do the opposite of the ostrich. We must go directly at what our buyers are looking for.

Although this mindset may seem counterintuitive at first, it's essential to your success. There will be moments when you and your team will debate:

> *"Should we say that online?"*
> *"Should we show that online?"*
> *"Should we sell that way?"*

In those moments, ask yourself, "Are we being the ostrich right now?" and "Would our buyers trust us more if we found a way to do this?" If the answer is yes, then act. Move away from the ostrich mindset and toward trust.

Understanding The 4 Pillars of a Known and Trusted Brand

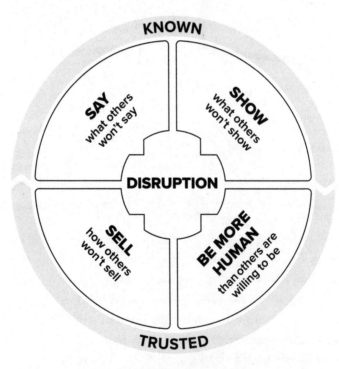

So what do we really mean when we say you have to be willing to do things others in your space aren't willing to do? Let's unpack each of the pillars to give you a better understanding of what we'll cover in each section of this book.

Pillar #1: Say What Others Aren't Willing to Say

Take a hard look at all your messaging and content online—your website, your social media, everything.

How much of it is truly unique? How much of it addresses topics most of your competitors shy away from discussing online?

In Chapter 4, you'll discover the five subjects buyers are obsessed with before making a purchase—subjects that most businesses are too afraid to address head-on, yet every buyer researches. These are known as **The Big 5,** and they've fueled significant lead and revenue growth for companies around the world that have implemented the Endless Customers methodology.

As you move through Section 2, you'll likely find yourself saying, "Wow, we've never talked about that online." I encourage you to look at each of these moments as a literal opportunity to become a more known and trusted brand. The only thing left is for your company to take action.

Pillar #2: Show What Others Aren't Willing to Show

How often do you hear businesses say, "We have a superior product," "We offer the best quality," or "We have the best people"?

All the time. And when everyone is making the same claims, it all starts to blend into one indistinguishable blur.

So how do you stand out in that sea of sameness? By showing what others aren't willing to show.

It's one thing to talk about your products, services, process, or people— it's a completely different thing to show them. Most companies hesitate to pull back the curtain because they're afraid of what might be seen. But that's *precisely* why transparency matters. The more you're willing to show, the more confident your customers become.

And when I say "show," I'm talking about **video.**

In Chapter 12, you'll discover the seven types of videos with the greatest impact on driving leads and sales, known as The **Selling 7.** You'll also gain access to actionable frameworks designed to help you create videos that generate more views, improve lead flow, and build a known and trusted brand.

Along the way, you'll see examples of companies bold enough to show what no one else is willing to—like Opes Partners, a property investment company in New Zealand that exploded their leads and sales by going all-in on video and showing what others in their market aren't willing to show.

Pillar #3: Sell in Ways Others Aren't Willing to Sell

Put yourself in the shoes of someone trying to buy from you, going through your sales process.

Forget for a moment all of the operational reasons why your sales process is the way it is, and pretend you're secretly shopping your business.

How would you feel? Is your process seamless? Or are there things that feel repetitive, frustrating, slow, unclear, or unnecessarily difficult?

Most businesses never ask these questions, and it shows. Their sales processes are stuck in old, rigid models—full of friction and frustration, costing millions in new business.

Now imagine flipping that experience entirely.

When you sell in ways others aren't willing to, your customers see you as different. You stand out. You become preferred. Your price point becomes easier to accept because buyers are paying for more than just a product—they're paying for a superior, frictionless experience.

And that's exactly what we'll discuss in Section 4. Here you'll discover the rise of the **seller-free economy,** a global shift where buyers demand more control over their journey. In Chapter 17, you'll learn the solution to this megatrend: **Self-Service Tools.** There, we'll explore the five types of self-service tools you need on your website to drive more trust, leads, and sales, including the growing importance of "self-pricing" tools.

And in Chapter 18, you'll learn how to craft the perfect **sales process** using content to dramatically increase closing rates, a technique called **Assignment Selling.**

Pillar #4: Be More Human in Ways Others Aren't Willing to Be

While technology is advancing at a pace that's hard to fathom, the world seems to be taking steps backward when it comes to building real human-to-human connections.

Let's remind ourselves of a simple truth: **People buy from people they trust.**

People trust those they can relate to. People with personality. People who understand their problems, who empathize with their situation, and who can help them avoid mistakes. People with perspective. People who stand for something. Those are the individuals we follow and engage with—not faceless, generic brands.

And while AI can be an incredible tool in your sales and marketing strategy (which we'll dive into in detail later), it's actually making this sense of disconnection even worse for many companies. Too many businesses misuse AI tools like ChatGPT, allowing the AI to churn out content without injecting their own stories or perspectives.

The result? Content that's not unique. Content your competitors could produce just as easily. Worse, it's robotic, stale, and boring. It lacks the elements that build real connections—authentic stories, unique perspectives, and personality. It's just noise.

But for your business, it doesn't have to be this way.

In Section 5, you'll discover:

- Why **personal brands,** not company brands, are the future of trust-building online.
- How to make your content truly look, sound, and feel human through **The Authentic 15**.
- The power of **one-to-one video** in the sales process to create a deeper, more authentic connection with your audience.
- The future of **digital avatars** and how these "digital humans" will transform the buying process.

As we close out the book, the final section is dedicated to helping you understand how to use The 4 Pillars of a Known and Trusted Brand to transform your business. In Chapters 25–27, the team at IMPACT will walk you through **The 5 Components of Endless Customers**—the more tactical implementation of what this mindset looks like when it's applied to your business. You'll learn how to put the principles of this book into action, continue to iterate and innovate, and ultimately become *the* disruptor and rule-maker in your market. By the end, you'll have the tools needed for implementation, prioritizing the work ahead, and tracking your progress.

And our promise to you? If you take the leap and commit to embracing transparency, rejecting outdated sales processes, and humanizing your brand in ways others aren't willing to, then you'll position your company to attract an endless flow of customers.

Reader's Resources: Visit the EC Companion Guide for additional information, visuals, and examples of The 4 Pillars of a Known and Trusted Brand.

Before we get into the first pillar, we need to address how search is changing and how AI-driven recommendations are rewriting the rules of visibility. To succeed, your business must consciously create the right signals to ensure the pillars deliver results.

3

Navigating the Era of Zero-Click

For decades now, search engine optimization (SEO) has been one of the most influential marketing tools of all time. Businesses became obsessed over keywords, backlinks, and search rankings. Many lived and died by search engine algorithms, chasing that coveted spot on Google's first page.

But a seismic shift is underway—the rise of zero-click searches. As businesses, if we're not prepared to adapt, we'll be left scrambling.

So, what is zero-click?

A **zero-click search** is when users get their answers right on the search results page without ever clicking through to a website.

Think about it: People search for "How tall is Mount Everest?" and, boom, the answer appears instantly. No clicks required. Google's aim has always been to deliver the best answer as fast as possible, and increasingly that answer doesn't even require a click. In fact, more than 50% of all Google searches end without a click.[1]

There are various studies done on zero-click, but all point to the same trend—more and more searches are ending in zero clicks. Today, it's estimated that the number of total searches that end in zero-click is around 62%, compared to 54% in the late 2010s.[2] In just a few short years, we've witnessed a drastic increase in zero-click searches.

For businesses, this trend means one thing: less traffic coming from Google. As more answers are delivered instantly, fewer people click through to websites. And this shift isn't slowing down—it's accelerating. Relying on organic search traffic as your primary lifeline is no longer sustainable.

The writing is on the wall: **You can no longer build your house on Google alone.**

The New Reality of Zero-Click

Google's continuous evolution toward zero-click isn't happening because they hate content creators or publishers. It's driven by user demand. People crave fast, convenient answers, and Google has perfected the art of giving them what they want—instantly.

If you're feeling the sting of declining website traffic, you're not alone. Many businesses have been blindsided by this shift. They've spent years perfecting their SEO strategy, only to watch their organic traffic nosedive. It's not because their content is bad. It's because Google (and AI) have changed the rules of the game. Even my swimming pool company's website, riverpoolsandspas.com—the most trafficked swimming pool website in the world—is seeing a decline in traffic coming from Google.

All of this means that the zero-click era is here, reshaping everything we know about online visibility. We've realized at River Pools that we simply can't afford to rely solely on traditional SEO strategies anymore for generating leads, and neither can your business. From here on out, your mission must evolve to **create signals, build a recognizable brand, and own your digital space in a way that both people and AI can't ignore.**

Why Signals Matter in a Zero-Click and AI-Driven World

Here's the uncomfortable question every business should be asking themselves: If users don't click to our website, how do we ensure they remember us?

The answer lies in creating **signals**—those unmissable, undeniable digital breadcrumbs that lead back to our brand, even if there's no direct click-through. This is why you must understand that every piece of content online you produce is a potential signal, not just to humans, but to AI as well.

When ChatGPT came out in 2022, most users didn't see it as a "recommendation" tool. But that changed quickly, and now its recommendations are affecting the success of brands and businesses worldwide. This means that if we're not on their radar, we run the risk of becoming invisible.

Not good.

Think of it this way: Even if a user doesn't visit your website, they can still absorb your brand messaging. You need to be unforgettable, even in a split-second encounter. Your brand must linger, resonate, and be recognizable, not just in a sea of information but also in the vast ocean of AI-driven recommendations.

How to Build a Brand That's Impossible for Humans and AI to Ignore

Because visibility doesn't guarantee clicks, brand building takes center stage as we look to the future. In many ways, that's exactly what this book is all about. Specifically, you must:

Dominate your niche with authority and credibility

Having your brand appear everywhere doesn't mean *anything* if you're not the trusted authority in your field. Google and AI systems alike prize authority, and so do your audience members. This means you need to double down on creating content that isn't just good, but unquestionably valuable—something you'll read all about in the coming chapters.

Ask yourself: How can we become synonymous with the solutions people are searching for?

This means creating content that is deep, thorough, and comprehensive, not surface-level and general. It means you must become the expert that's quoted, referenced, and seen as the source of knowledge. You must think beyond ranking for keywords, and instead think about being the name people and algorithms associate with the topic. Again, this book will show you exactly how to do this.

Elevate your content to build awareness

You need to create content not just for SEO, but even more so for brand awareness. The content you produce should serve multiple purposes—It should educate, entertain, and (most importantly) stick with people. It should include original research, thoughtful analysis, and aim to add something new to the conversation.

Remember, it's not just people consuming this content. AI tools and systems are absorbing, learning, and choosing what to promote. Your content needs to be optimized to signal both human relevance and AI importance. Keywords matter, yes, but what matters most is the overall context, depth, and quality of your message.

Utilize platform-specific strategies

No two platforms operate the same way, and if you're treating your approach to content as a one-size-fits-all, you're likely going to struggle.

Zero-click also means more people are discovering brands on platforms like YouTube, LinkedIn, TikTok, Instagram, and many others. These platforms don't rely on clicks to drive engagement—they focus on the brand experience.

Although this book isn't a deep dive on all things social media, the principles taught here should be foundational to your social media content efforts. As you create content for social media, design it to start conversations. Think about the native features of each platform and use them to your advantage. LinkedIn might be perfect for sparking insightful discussion, while Instagram can showcase your brand's behind-the-scenes culture.

And remember: AI algorithms on these platforms are constantly learning. The more engaging your content, the more likely it is to be recommended.

Build brand equity with consistency and frequency

Ever heard of the "rule of seven"? It's the marketing principle that states people need to hear or see your brand at least seven times before it starts to stick. These days, that number is likely much higher. Zero-click has made this rule even more important. Your audience may not click through to your website, but if they see you everywhere, consistently showing up and adding value, your brand starts to occupy space in their minds—and AI algorithms notice you, too.

Frequency matters. It's not just about quality; it's about being there, again and again, to drive home your message. This means having a consistent publishing schedule and showing up where your audience spends their time.

The Path Forward: Redefining Success Metrics Beyond "Website Traffic"

We need to stop defining success solely by website traffic. Yes, that's still important, but if we hang our entire strategy on traffic alone, we're potentially doomed.

Instead, we should focus on metrics like brand mentions, social engagement, and whether we're being recommended by AI systems. Are people talking about us? Are they sharing our content? Are we the go-to source for AI-driven recommendations?

You're not just competing for clicks; you're competing for memory. The brands that will thrive in the era of zero-click and AI are the ones that aren't just selling products or services. They're creating movements, they're disrupting, and they're building loyal communities—something you'll read about in the chapters ahead.

You're playing a long game here. Brand-building isn't an overnight thing, but it's what will keep your company thriving in the new digital landscape. **If your brand is recognizable, trusted, and top-of-mind for people and AI, you'll win—even if you're not winning in clicks.**

Reader's Resources: Looking for additional guidance on the right metrics to be tracking for your business and your implementation of the Endless Customer System? Check out the EC Companion guide for more information.

Zero-click is a disruptor, but it's also an opportunity. It's pushing us to become better and more thoughtful with our sales and marketing strategies.

As you read ahead about The 4 Pillars of a Known and Trusted Brand and learn about the power of industry disruption, you'll discover a clear and proven system designed to make sure you're taking advantage of the zero-click opportunity by driving massive signals to your potential customers and AI alike, ultimately building you into one of the most known and trusted brands in your market.

2 | Say What Others Aren't Willing to Say

Words have power.

They shape perceptions, influence decisions, and build trust—or destroy it. Yet too often businesses shy away from saying what buyers truly want to hear. Whether it's because of fear, tradition, or simply not knowing what to say, most companies fall silent on the very topics their customers care about most.

This is why the first pillar of becoming a known and trusted brand is simple: **Say what others aren't willing to say.**

Buyers today demand transparency, honesty, and answers to their burning questions. They want to know the cost, the problems, the comparisons, and the reviews—essentially everything that will help them feel confident in their decisions. But instead of finding these answers, many buyers are met with vague messaging, silence, or companies that hope they'll pick up the phone to ask.

Today, that's not how trust is built.

In this section, we'll explore how embracing radical transparency can transform the way your business communicates. You'll learn about the foundational power of **The Big 5**—the core topics all buyers research—and how saying what others won't can turn your content into a trust-building machine. Along the way, we'll share real-world examples of businesses that dared to step outside their comfort zones and, as a result, became the most known and trusted brand in their markets.

By the end of this section, you'll understand the topics your company needs to be addressing and have the tools to say what your buyers are already asking—and in doing so, create a foundation of trust that leads to more sales, more loyalty, and, ultimately, more customers.

4 | The Big 5

It's a story we've heard many times. As businesses, we're creating content, publishing articles, and making videos—yet the needle isn't moving. Why aren't our marketing efforts generating qualified leads (or any leads at all)? Is the stuff we're doing actually working and helping to generate revenue? And why doesn't AI recommend us? How can we get humans and AI alike to take notice?

More than 90% of the time, the reason is clear: **Companies aren't talking about what buyers want to know.**

And what do buyers want to know? Every question. Every fear. Every concern. When they're searching for this information online, that's what they're trying to figure out.

The problem is, most companies start by creating content for "casual lookers"—those people still far from making a buying decision—or worse, for people who aren't even in the market at all.

This is not the right strategy. Content targeting casual browsers will take much longer to yield measurable results and not drive the sales opportunities you need.

So how do you get your content to generate real sales opportunities right now, and not in a year from now?

You flip the strategy. You start creating content for actual buyers—people who already know they're in the market for what you offer and are closest to purchasing. By addressing their very specific questions, worries, fears, objections, and so on—you're not only giving buyers exactly what they want, but you're doing the same for AI.

When companies address these topics openly and honestly, they drive more leads and sales than any other subject matter. We call these topics **The Big 5,** and once you learn about them, you'll realize two things:

1. The Big 5 are the literal epitome of "Say what others aren't willing to say."
2. You've inherently always known that you should be addressing these five subjects with your content, as they represent exactly how *you* research online.

So, what are The Big 5?

The Big 5

Think about the process you go through as a buyer when you're seriously considering a product, service, or company—especially a significant purchase. What do you always find yourself researching before you reach out to a business or make any buying decision?

First and foremost, you're probably thinking about price, right? The first question on your mind is likely "How much is this going to cost me?"

But it doesn't stop there.

Once you've seen the price, you start digging deeper. What makes the price go up or down? What do others say about it? Have people had good experiences, or are there any red flags?

You scroll through reviews, looking for real-life feedback—both positive and negative. You're trying to gauge if this is really worth your time and money, or if you're about to make a mistake.

Sound familiar?

We all follow a similar process when we buy something of significance. Whether or not we realize it, we tend to research the same five key subject areas before making a decision. These five subjects have become so consistent that they're known as **The Big 5,** and long before big brands understood what they were, practitioners of *They Ask, You Answer* (now *Endless Customers*) were well-informed about their stunning influence on the world of search.

The Big Five

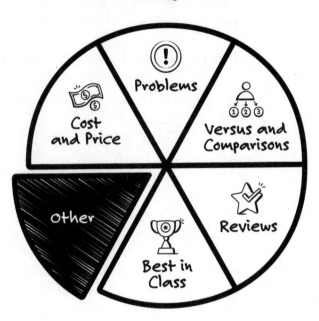

Here's what they are:

1. **Cost and Price:** Everyone wants to know what they can expect to pay. They also want to understand what constitutes "value." Such behavior is universal among *all* buyers.
2. **Problems:** A desire to buy something is often accompanied by fears and worries. What are the drawbacks? How could this purchase go wrong?
3. **Versus and Comparisons:** We love to compare. It's how we make informed decisions, stacking one option against another to find the best solution for our needs.
4. **Reviews:** We want the good, the bad, and the ugly. And importantly, we want to know who a product or service *is*, and *is not*, a good fit for.
5. **Best in Class:** We search for the "best," "most," "top," or whatever extreme we can find. Even though we might not end up buying the "best," we at least want to be able to have a clear sense of our full suite of options.

Think about the last time you shopped on Amazon. Whether you were buying a new gadget, a kitchen appliance, or even this book, chances are you found yourself scanning for answers to the same questions—questions that fall squarely into The Big 5.

As Amazon has improved their product pages over time, they've mastered the art of addressing each of these key areas seamlessly, showing almost a perfect example of what Endless Customer content should look like:

- The price? It's always up front and center.
- Problems? You'll see them covered in the Q&A sections where customers share their real-world experiences, highlighting any cons, issues, or disappointments with the product.
- Want to compare? Amazon provides side-by-side product comparisons with alternatives.
- And those reviews? Thousands of them, often unfiltered, letting you know exactly what to expect—both the good and the bad. And now, thanks to AI, it takes things one step further to highlight the top problems and issues shared across reviews.
- Finally, if you're looking for the best-rated product, you'll find badges that call out the "Top Choice" or "Best Seller."

All of The Big 5 are there, working together to answer the questions Amazon knows matter most to their customers.

Have you ever made a first-time purchase on Amazon without thoroughly scanning these elements? Probably not. Sure, with repeat or impulse buys, we're quicker to drop something into our cart. But when it's something new—especially something pricey or when it's an important decision—we don't take chances.

Amazon gets it, and that's why they're the most successful retailer in history.

You can create your product and service pages just like Amazon structures theirs. This way, The Big 5 are all there, and buyers can find exactly what they're looking for, quickly. Done correctly, this offers a user experience your website visitors have clearly never experienced with your competitors and builds massive trust in the process.

Say What Others Aren't Willing to Say

Want to know what's fascinating about The Big 5? Even though when you go to buy something you're obsessed with these topics, **these are the very topics most businesses *avoid* talking about.**

Whether it's on their websites, social platforms, or You Tube, they're too scared to address the elephant in the room. Sadly, instead of giving buyers what they want, they'd rather be like the ostrich, sticking their heads in the sand, avoiding having to talk about them until they're in a conversation with the prospect—which is too late.

Not smart.

Especially in an age when every answer is at our fingertips.

When you fail to address these key topics online, where buyers are doing their research, you essentially force potential customers to look elsewhere—likely at one of your competitors.

And I don't know about you, but that's not something I'm interested in doing.

When I wrote *They Ask, You Answer*, The Big 5 was primarily discussed from the context of written content. Since then, we've continually seen The Big 5 come to life and be just as powerful—if not more so—when also applied to other mediums, such as video, podcasts, and social media. In fact, leading companies that implement The Big 5 have successfully integrated multiple channels into their content strategies.

Now, knowing you may have your doubts about The Big 5, let's explore each of them in detail.

5 | Topic 1: Cost and Price

To understand the psychology of discussing cost and price online, let's first examine our own behavior as buyers. As we proceed, you must be honest with yourself and consider your typical online actions, because in many ways this is an exercise in self-awareness.

When you're on a website looking for cost and price information and you can't find it, what emotion do you experience?

Frustration, right? That's what we refer to as the "F-word of the internet."

And what gives you the right at this moment to feel so frustrated?

Because you're the buyer. You're literally trying to give this company your money, but they are making it very difficult for you to do so, aren't they?

In that moment of frustration, do you keep looking on the website until you find pricing information?

Of course not. In fact, we've found most website visitors will leave a website in less than 10 seconds if they're looking for cost and price information and can't find what they're looking for.

Or better yet, in that moment of frustration, do you as the searcher say to yourself, "Of course they're not discussing pricing online—they're a *value-based business*. I'm going to call them on the phone instead"?

Not a chance. In fact, that's laughable, isn't it? This is because, as someone who is seeking information, your natural reaction is to simply keep searching.

And you search until what happens?

Until you find what you're looking for.

And generally speaking, whichever company is willing to give you what you're looking for (pricing information in this case), what are they going to get from you?

That's right, your business.

And even if they don't get your business, the one that gave you the information is the one you're going to reach out to first.

If we were to break down the core reason we get so upset, though, it's because we (as the customer) know that they (as the business) know the answer. And because we know they know the answer (or could at least give us a better sense of the answer), and they're not giving it to us, we now feel like they're *hiding* something from us.

And the moment you feel like anyone is hiding anything from you online, what happens?

Trust is gone.

And as we stated from the very beginning of this book, trust is the business we're all in.

Now, the most important question I want to ask you next is:

Do you openly discuss the cost and price of your product or service on your website and online right now?

If you're like most companies, especially those in B2B, you do not. And chances are, if you don't, you're probably trying to justify the reasons why you don't at this very moment as you read this.

I've talked to thousands of businesses about why they don't discuss pricing on their website or in the content they produce online. When I ask them why, I tend to get one (or more) of the following three reasons. They might phrase it differently, but it typically boils down to three main objections:

Objection #1: Every solution is complex. Our prices vary. It depends.

When was the last time you visited a website, couldn't find pricing information, and thought, "Of course they can't show prices. There are just too many variables"?

Probably never.

Consumers know that prices vary, but they still want you to give them a range or an estimate, because at a minimum, they want a general idea of what they can expect to spend. When it comes to pricing, what matters most isn't that you provide an exact number. What matters most is that you explain *why* it depends and how it can vary.

In other words, what drives cost up (across the industry) for your product or service? What drives cost down? Why are some companies so expensive? Why are others so cheap? And where, generally speaking, does the price range of your products/services fall?

Objection #2: If we discuss pricing, our competitors will find out what we charge.

This is one of the most laughable justifications for not discussing cost online. Why? Because if I were to ask any experienced salesperson on your team if they have a good sense of how much your competitors charge, what would they say?

Of course, they would know.

So if you can guess how much your competitors are charging, then that means your competitors also know what *you* charge—or at a minimum, they have a very good sense about how much you charge.

In other words, when it comes to pricing, there are very few secrets in an industry, and most informed companies have at least a decent sense about what everyone else is charging.

Objection #3: We'll scare customers away.

Some businesses fear they'll scare buyers if they talk about pricing on their website. But, as we've learned, the thing that *actually* scares buyers away isn't when a company takes the time to educate them and teach them value, but rather when they *don't* talk about it, or they hide it.

In other words, when it comes to your potential customers online, ignorance is *not* bliss. Rather, ignorance breeds doubt. And doubt breeds inaction. And inaction breeds a lack of leads. And leads, as you know, are the lifeline of any business.

Of course, businesses use other arguments (although they're not as common) about why they can't address cost and price online:

- **We don't sell direct.** Sure, this may be true, but it's a conversation happening in your industry and therefore needs to be addressed. Some of our wildest case studies around pricing come from manufacturers, as well as others that don't sell directly to consumers.

Remember, every industry needs someone to lead the conversation and define value, otherwise a lack of education will always lead to commoditization.

- **Legal and/or regulatory considerations won't allow it.** This is a very common excuse, especially in the financial services space. But despite the fact that we've heard objections many times, there's never been an instance where the company couldn't actually address the question.

  Remember, you don't have to *answer* the question of cost. But you do have to *address* the question of cost. This is where trust is built.

- **We do value-based selling.** If this is true, it's all the more reason to address the topic of cost upfront. Too often, businesses wait until the prospect questions the price or proposal before they explain the value of what they offer. Unfortunately, by holding off until the final stages of the buyer's journey, many prospects never even reach the proposal stage and they miss out on the essential education needed to make a value-based buying decision.

  Again, I can't stress this point enough: If you choose *not* to educate your market on the pricing of your product or service, then you will literally *commoditize* the thing you sell.

- **We need opportunities to negotiate.** When a company makes this statement, it's generally a clear sign their sales process is stuck in a pre-internet mindset where they assume buyers won't find pricing information elsewhere online.

Never underestimate your customers' ability to find the information they need online. If they want it, they'll get it—so it's in your best interest to make sure they get it from you. And if your reasoning is simply "We need room to negotiate," that's a sign that you may not have the buyer's best interests at heart—seriously undermining your credibility as a trusted brand in the information age. Furthermore, keep in mind that giving a price range still gives you flexibility.

How One Article Generated More Than $35M in Sales

In 2009, amid a worldwide recession, my partners and I at River Pools were desperate to save the business. It was during this time we became truly obsessed with what buyers wanted online and decided to become the best teachers in the world when it came to fiberglass swimming pools.

As with most products or services, just about anyone who called us interested in a pool asked the same question: *"I'm not going to hold you to it, but could you at least give me a feel for how much something like this is going to cost?"*

Most businesses—certainly those that offer a product or service that has a price range—loathe this question from prospects. Historically, the preferred approach has been to ignore the question around price as long as possible, pushing first to do your entire "pitch" before giving the buyer a sense of how much it will cost.

But if you look at the way you shop today, this idea of holding back pricing is the last thing you want as a buyer. And I knew our pool shoppers were no different. Yet despite this, no swimming pool company in the world at that time had addressed the subject of pricing on their website.

In other words, they were all the ostrich. Why? Because they were afraid of the same three things we discussed earlier, using these classic excuses:

- Every job is different and it depends.
- We don't want our competitors to learn about our pricing.
- If a prospect sees we're more expensive, then we'll scare them away.

Falling back on the belief that we needed to be willing to say what others in our space weren't willing to say, we decided to fully explain the cost of building a fiberglass swimming pool on our website—becoming the first company in the world to do so.

And how did we do it without backing ourselves in a pricing corner? Simple.

We approached the article as an opportunity to educate our buyers, not to give them an exact price. We related the process of buying a fiberglass pool to that of buying a car: many options, accessories, and so on, listing each one, offering a true sense of the potential scope of a project.

After that, we discussed the different types of options and packages typically offered by pool builders, like patios, fencing, landscaping, covers, and heaters. Furthermore, we explained why some swimming pool companies were so cheap and others so expensive, giving the reader a very clear understanding of both the cost and the *value* of an inground swimming pool.

What was the result of putting such an article out to the world? In one word, extraordinary.

"How Much Does a Fiberglass Pool Cost?" Article ROI

After publishing the article to our website, conversations with leads/prospects started to sound different. People would call in and say things like "I just want to thank you for being so open and willing to talk about how much a pool costs. I really had no idea what to expect."

In other words, the trust our potential customers felt toward us was growing dramatically, all because we weren't the ostrich and didn't shy away from addressing a question that was so important to each of them to understand.

But what happened next was even more stunning.

Within days, leads started coming in, driving more qualified, productive conversations. These leads led to more sales appointments, and those appointments eventually equated to revenue.

And we're not talking about a little bit of revenue.

In fact, because we use a tool like HubSpot that helps us measure the return on investment (ROI) of our marketing efforts, we know that this article has now generated millions of views, thousands of sales appointments, and at this point more than $35 million in sales.

All from an article that took me 45 minutes to write at my kitchen table. Talk about ROI.

That one single article saved our company and lifted us out of bankruptcy, sparking years of growth and incredible prosperity.

And do you know what's funny?

We never actually said exactly how much a fiberglass pool costs. Why? Because you can't give an exact answer. But you can address the question in such a way that deeply educates the buyer and helps them get a clear sense of what to expect.

To this day, addressing cost and price on your website is still one of the most powerful trust and lead generators you can make. We've seen it produce tremendous results over and over again. Yet most businesses still shy away from it.

Hopefully now, though, your mind has shifted and you're able to see why discussing pricing could be so powerful for your business.

In this next section, we'll make it even easier for you by breaking down "The Perfect Pricing Page."

How to Create "The Perfect Pricing Page"

Our team at IMPACT has helped hundreds of companies create on their website what we call, "The Perfect Pricing Page." **We've compiled a list of the most common pricing-related questions,** and although not all of these apply to every industry, they do apply to most:

1. What drives costs in an industry up?
2. What drives costs in an industry down?
3. What makes some companies so expensive?
4. What makes some companies so cheap?
5. Where do *your* prices fall (range)?
6. Explain variations in industry packaging.
7. Explain lifetime cost versus initial price.
8. Show financing as part of the cost conversation.
9. Show examples (visually) with corresponding price ranges.
10. List the pricing-related frequently asked questions (FAQs).
11. Include charts, graphs, and the like.
12. What are the historical pricing trends?
13. Is it (really) worth it?

Although each of these is very helpful to anyone learning about pricing, the most important ones to discuss in order to teach "value" are the first five. Let's look at each of these in a little more depth:

1. **What drives the cost up for your product/service?** Buyers want to understand what they'll be paying for. Whether it's the

quality of materials, additional services, or unique features, from an industry perspective explain the factors that drive the cost up of your product or service.

2. **What drives costs down?** What factors cause the price or your product or service to decrease? Are there ways to offer a more affordable solution? Are there alternative options or more efficient processes? This transparency empowers buyers to make an informed choice, knowing what they'll sacrifice in terms of quality or service to save money.

3. **Why are some companies so expensive?** Don't leave buyers guessing why some companies charge more. Explain the reasons why some companies are higher-priced—differences in the product or service, specializations, different premium materials used, warranties—so buyers can decide if those extras are worth it.

4. **Why are some companies so cheap?** We hear this all the time: "I can't put pricing on my site because my competition charges way less." Our response: "Why are they cheaper?" The answer often involves overseas manufacturing, lower quality, or lackluster service. Buyers often make poor decisions, choosing the cheapest option not because they're price-motivated, but because they didn't know any better. No one educated them. That's where you come in.

5. **Where, roughly, does your company's pricing fall?** Be clear about where your pricing stands in the industry and, most importantly, why. Did you make a deliberate decision about quality? Is that reflected in your pricing? Help buyers understand what they're getting for the price and why you stand out in the market.

This format for how to discuss cost and price works great on any medium. So whether you're discussing pricing in an article, video, or audio—following "The Perfect Pricing Page" format ensures the prospect is now thoroughly educated and truly has a great sense as to what to expect.

One other important suggestion about explaining pricing online: Most industries have different "tiers" of pricing—think of it almost from a low-end, mid-tier, and high-end perspective. Using different tiers as a means of explaining how pricing works within an industry is very helpful to potential buyers, and something that has been incredibly effective for many of the clients we've worked with across various industries.

The Future of Online Pricing Is Here

Ultimately, it is my great hope that this chapter has helped you realize just how possible (and easy) it is to explain pricing in your industry. As I mentioned before, pricing is the clearest example of being willing to say what others in your industry aren't willing to say, laying the foundation of a known and trusted brand.

Having worked with so many large and small brands to help them effectively address this subject, I *know* that what you've read in this chapter works. The data behind it is empirical.

Now it just requires action—as well as not overthinking the subject of addressing pricing online, something we see too many companies and brands suffer from.

The great thing, though, is that we're just scratching the surface with respect to this subject. Later in the book, you'll learn more about what the future of online pricing will look like—from online self-pricing tools (also known as pricing estimators) to digital avatars that will give real-time quotes to website visitors. There's a lot more to discuss in those chapters.

6

Topic 2: Problems

As buyers, we worry more about what could go wrong than what can go right. We want to know the good and the bad—both sides of the coin.

But if we're being honest, we're mostly concerned with the bad.

Going back to Amazon, for example, when you're browsing reviews, are you only clicking on the five-star reviews to see how much people love a product?

Probably not. You're more likely focused on the one-star reviews, hunting for the horror stories, trying to figure out what could go wrong if you buy it.

Yet, as businesses, we typically *avoid* addressing these subjects. It comes down to a psychological issue that almost all businesses struggle with, and that's the concept of **addressing the elephant in the room,** or the perceived "negatives" of our product or service. This means we try not to shine a light on any objection, worry, fear, or concern a potential buyer might have with our offerings.

And as buyers, what do we think we're going to find in those one-star reviews?

Yep, it's the negative. But it's critical that we, as buyers, find it.

So instead of forcing your potential customers to find it, *why not give it to them?*

I actually refer to this principle of showing both sides (the pros and cons of a purchase) as the **Law of the Coin,** because every coin has two sides, and so does every purchase. There are reasons someone should buy something. And there are reasons they should not buy it.

As a business, this gives you a choice. You can allow the consumer to discover your elephant(s) themselves, and not learn them from you. Or you can address the question head-on and say, "Here's our elephant. It's important you know this before making a decision."

The savvy and informed buyers of today will do whatever it takes to find both sides of this "coin" during their buyer's journey, which is *exactly* why the smartest companies that best understand trust are quick to show the potential pros and cons of any product or service they sell, using this Law of the Coin.

And if you are willing to do this, not only will you surprise potential customers with your radical transparency, but they will quickly sense that you're not like the rest of the companies they've researched. They'll see that you care more about them making an informed, correct decision than you care about making a sale.

Once this is accomplished, you've "disarmed" the prospect, allowing them to drop their guard and being to trust you in ways they wouldn't have otherwise been able to do.

As a business in the digital age, you must accept this truth: **Buyers aren't dumb**.

Sure, they may start off uninformed, but they will not remain ignorant, especially with the access to AI that they now have.

In every industry we've worked with, we've seen clear patterns of doubts, fears, objections, issues, worries, and concerns that potential customers have, and these are precisely the "problems" they're researching when making a purchasing decision. When we show clients what their buyers are searching for, they're often shocked at the sheer number of unique doubts their potential customers have. These questions (or real-life concerns) usually start with phrases like:

> *Is it true that. . .*
> *Your competitor told me that. . .*
> *I hear there were issues with. . .*
> *I'm worried about. . .*

Consider for a moment how many times someone on your sales team has had to address these objections. Do they know exactly what to say? Does your company have a shared doctrine in terms of the right response? Are they resolving the concern or planting more seeds of doubt?

This is why it's your job to become incredibly familiar with all the doubts and objections a potential customer might have with your product, service, or industry, and address each one to the best of your ability—once again *saying* what others in your space aren't willing to say.

And remember: **The greatest way in life to resolve a concern is to address it before it becomes a concern.** By proactively addressing potential problems, you build trust and position yourself as a transparent, reliable source of information in your industry.

What Could Go Wrong with Metal Roofs?

One of our clients, Sheffield Metals—a metal roofing manufacturer based in the Midwest—provides an excellent example of understanding buyer concerns. They recognize that investing in a metal roof is a significant decision. For someone new to metal roofing, it's natural to wonder about potential problems that might come with this type of roofing material.

Instead of shying away from this potentially intimidating topic, the team at Sheffield Metals decided to address the elephant in the room head on in their article, "Metal Roofing Problems: 7 Common Issues That Could Affect Your Roof."

They open up the article by saying: "No product in the world is perfect, no matter how much money it's worth or how well it's cared for. You could be in a lucky situation where nothing ever goes wrong with something you've purchased, or you could experience one or more problems at any given time. It all just depends. Metal roofing is no different."

They go on to cover the top seven common problems that could occur with a metal roof, potential ways and methods to remedy or avoid the problem, and important considerations to keep in mind that'll help bypass some problems. The article is incredibly thorough and gives a homeowner everything they need to consider before purchasing a metal roof.

Sheffield Metals is even bold enough to say that a metal roof is not for everyone, even though metal roofing is the only type of roof they sell. This is incredibly trust-inducing for any potential customer to hear, because rarely do brands openly admit, "Hey, we're not the best fit for everyone." But when brands embrace this transparency, it empowers buyers while saving everyone involved more time—a clear win-win.

Taking it one step further, Sheffield Metals also created a supporting video entitled "7 Common Problems of a Metal Roof," published it to YouTube, and embedded it in the article. As of today, this article has received more than a million views, with the corresponding video having more than half a million views on YouTube. It has had a tremendous effect on their brand for homeowners and contractors around the country.

It's no surprise the Sheffield Metals brand has made a massive leap within their industry in a short period of time, exploding sales and profitability along the way.

They are known, they are trusted, and they are winning.

Mission accomplished.

7

Topic 3: Versus and Comparisons

Think about how many times you've gone online to compare one thing against another.

Hundreds, right?

As buyers, we're obsessed with comparisons. We want to know the best, the worst, and everything in between. With all the information at our fingertips, this thirst for comparison has only grown.

Consider your last major purchase. Did you look at only one option?

Probably not. Most buyers stack up multiple products or services against each other before making a decision. And it's not just you—millions of comparisons are searched online every day.

At IMPACT, we've worked with countless companies on their journey to become the most trusted brand in their market, and comparison content has consistently been a top performer over the last decade.

Let's look at the example of RetroFoam, a home foam insulation provider with dealers across the U.S. For years, home insulation was dominated by two products: cellulose and fiberglass—the stuff you find in rolls.

Then, RetroFoam introduced injection-based insulation.

For a while, RetroFoam's growth was slower than expected—until they embraced the principles of the Endless Customers System and leaned into what others in the insulation space weren't willing to do: answer the tough comparison questions.

One of the most common questions homeowners were researching was *What's the difference between spray foam, fiberglass, and cellulose insulation?*

Even though this question was being asked prolifically, most contractors refused to answer it online. Why? Because they were thinking like ostriches— afraid that mentioning alternative choices would cost them business. It sounds ridiculous, but that's how many businesses still think today—maybe even yours.

RetroFoam, however, didn't bury their heads in the sand. They tackled *every* comparison question potential customers had, like:

> *"What's the best insulation for an attic (spray foam versus fiberglass versus cellulose)?"*
> *"Foam insulation versus fiberglass: a comprehensive comparison to coffee cups."*
> *"What's the difference between RetroFoam injection foam and spray foam insulation?"*

And they didn't just stop at answering the questions—they did it exceptionally well.

When speaking to audiences about comparison content, we often hear the same objection: "Isn't it impossible to come across as unbiased? Buyers don't want our opinion because they assume it'll be biased."

This is a myth.

In fact, you can easily disprove it by asking your sales team: *Has a prospect ever asked you to compare our product or service with a competitor's?* And 99.9% of the time, the answer is *yes.* Your customers *want* to know your opinion on comparison questions. And if they're asking, it's your job to answer.

But here's the key: You must answer in a way that's honest, unbiased, and shows both sides of the coin.

RetroFoam excels at this. Take their article "What is the Best Insulation for an Attic? Spray Foam versus Fiberglass versus Cellulose" as an example. RetroFoam starts off by acknowledging their expertise in spray and injection foam insulation, but they also point out their knowledge of traditional attic insulations like fiberglass and cellulose.

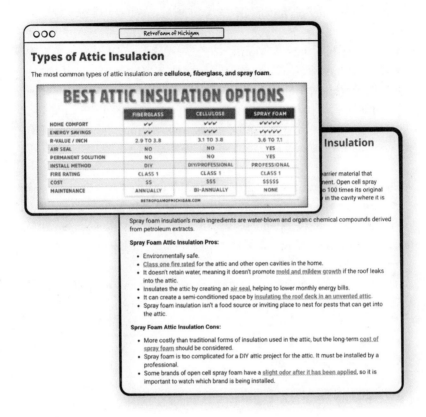

Then they share a graphic comparing all three options, followed by:

"As you can see from the image above, there are some differences in the benefits these materials have to offer. Let's take a closer look at each material to see which will be best for your attic's needs."

This opening uses a principle we've applied with countless clients, which we call **disarmament**—communicating in a way that drops the reader's guard and builds immediate trust.

The best way to disarm an audience online is by telling them something unexpected. RetroFoam knows that honestly addressing the elephant in the room builds an immediate sense of trust.

Here's how they do it:

- They openly state they only sell spray foam insulation.
- They admit spray foam isn't the best choice for everyone.
- They acknowledge that fiberglass or cellulose might be better in some situations.
- They explain the pros and cons of each option, allowing readers to decide for themselves.

Once again, RetroFoam has disarmed the prospect by effectively using the Law of the Coin. And because RetroFoam gave buyers exactly what they wanted—honesty, openness, and helpful information—they've built one of the most trusted brands in North America for home insulation.

You can do the same with your business.

It starts with identifying the comparison-based questions your customers are asking. The most common types of comparison questions include:

- Your product versus another product
- Option versus option
- Accessory versus accessory
- Company versus company
- Methodology versus methodology

The list goes on, but you get the idea.

The bottom line? Buyers *love* to compare, and that will never change.

So lead the conversation—or someone else will.

8

Topic 4: Reviews

Reviews have become a staple of how we research, how we buy, and our entire economy. Rarely do we make a purchase without first exploring reviews. Whether it's Amazon, Google, Yelp, or Reddit, we want to know what kind of experiences other real people and real customers had with the thing we want to buy.

But when it comes to reviews, we don't just want to read about the good, the five stars, the people who had the perfect experience. Sure, that matters, but the moment we get very serious about buying or doing business with someone we then turn our attention to the *bad* reviews (the Law of the Coin we mentioned earlier).

As buyers, we want to know:

> *What went wrong?*
> *Who is it not a good fit for?*
> *Were any mistakes made?*
> *What happened when there was a problem?*
> *How did the company/brand respond when there was an issue?*

Despite the fact most companies realize how important reviews are, most make three major mistakes when it comes to reviews:

1. They don't have an intentional plan in place to generate more reviews from their customers.
2. They don't believe they should be creating reviews about their own services/products.
3. When they do create reviews, they make the mistake of coming across as biased, mainly because they're not following the Law of the Coin.

Let's take a brief look at each.

Get Intentional About Reviews

As you recall from Chapter 3, much of our success in an AI-driven search world depends heavily on our ability to create more signals in the marketplace that point to our business and essentially tell AI, "Hey, this is a company you should be recommending."

This is one major reason reviews are so incredibly important. Reviews play a critical role in how AI evaluates businesses. Rest assured, AI will factor in platforms like Google Reviews when determining whether to recommend a business.

If your company doesn't already have a plan for getting reviews—or worse, if you barely have any reviews at all—it's time to fix that. AI is watching, and so are your future customers.

But here's the thing: This isn't about begging or bribing for five stars. It's about creating real opportunities for your customers to share their honest experiences—and making it ridiculously easy for them to do so.

Here are some essential tips on how to generate more reviews for your business:

Ask—Every Single Time

This sounds obvious, but most companies don't ask for reviews consistently. Make it part of the sales process to ask for a review immediately after delivering the product or service. And whatever you do, *do not wait*. Strike while the iron is hot, and don't consider the deal done until you've gotten that review.

Automate the request

Depending on your business and your ability to ask directly, consider sending automated follow-up emails or text messages post-purchase, inviting customers to share their experience. Tools like Google My Business and Yelp even let you link directly to your review page. Take advantage of this and remove *all* friction.

Incentivize (without bribing)

Offering a small perk—a discount on their next purchase or any other small token of appreciation—can motivate people to leave feedback. Just be careful; you don't want to only push positive reviews. People can smell dishonesty from a mile away.

Make it easy

People won't jump through hoops. Send a direct link, give clear instructions, and even show an example of a past review. The easier and simpler you make it, the more responses you'll get.

Respond to existing reviews

This is critical, and a lot of companies overlook this entirely. Whether it's a glowing endorsement or a not-so-nice critique, respond thoughtfully. Potential customers vetting you in the future will be very much paying attention to how honestly and sincerely you engage with negative reviews online—so use these as an opportunity to build more trust.

Showcase your reviews

Showcase reviews on your website, on social media, in your newsletter, or even in your actual location. When customers see their voices being highlighted, they're more likely to join in. If you've ever been to a Five Guys restaurant, you've seen a classic example of someone showcasing reviews unlike anyone else in their space. In fact, they built a worldwide brand by plastering customers reviews in all their bathrooms, giving customers a sense of "Wow, everyone *loves* this place!"

One note about showing reviews: The more you're able to show actual images or videos of the person leaving the review—the more "real" the review becomes, something we'll explore further in the "show" pillar.

Create Your Own Product Reviews

When our team works with a business selling any type of product, one of the first sets of videos we always have them produce are product review videos.

Why is this? Because product review videos have incredible utility. They can be used in a litany of ways across your entire marketing and sales efforts, including your website, social, YouTube, direct email to prospects, and more.

Sadly, many companies just leave it up to sites like Amazon and influencers on YouTube to review their products. But leaving your fate solely in the hands of a third-party website is a very bad idea. Take control—you need to own all conversations online about whatever it is you sell.

What Does the Perfect Review Look Like?

If you're going to create review content (text, video, audio) of your own products or services, it's absolutely essential that you always follow the Law of the Coin that we previously mentioned:

- Talk very clearly about who your solution *is* a good fit for.
- Talk very clearly about who your solution *is not* a good fit for.

And remember, don't be sarcastic or snarky when discussing the "cons" or negatives of a product. Be real, be honest, and allow the trust to build.

A great example of this comes from Greg Knighton, founder of BTOD.com (Beyond the Office Door). About a decade ago, Greg was attempting to start an office furniture ecommerce company when he attended one of my talks. At the time, he was just getting started and was struggling to generate leads and sales. He was desperate to get noticed and become more known in the market.

His solution? He went all-in with video, embraced transparency in ways no one in office furniture had ever done before, and everything took off from there.

One major catalyst to Greg's company's growth and sustained success is his deep understanding of reviews, and how he utilizes them in various ways to build a brand. If you check out the website at BTOD.com and BTODtv YouTube channel, you'll find:

1. The BTOD.com homepage prominently showcases that they have more than 3,200 reviews on Trustpilot and a TrustScore of 4.8. That's a *lot* of reviews, and quite a powerful "signal" to visitors, verifying that it's a trustworthy company to work with.

2. BTOD.com has an extremely active review solicitation program from all their customers. On various pages of their website, they show multiple, real-time reviews that have come in from Trustpilot. Furthermore, 100% of the products they sell on their site have a review score shown with it.

3. On their BTODtv YouTube channel, they've done multiple types of product review videos, including:

> *"We Picked the Best Office Chair for EVERY Price"*
> *"I Tested 1-Star Office Chairs"*
> *"Herman Miller Mirror 2 Ergonomic Chair Review"*
> *"I Picked the Most Comfortable Office Chair for the Lowest Price"*
> *"Herman Miller Sayl Review: My Opinion 1 Year Later"*

Their YouTube page has many more examples we could mention (along with *millions* of views), but hopefully you see just how diverse and unique review content can be. Platforms like YouTube and consumers love a little bit of creativity, and BTOD.com does just that with all their unique review styles.

And just to give you a final sense of the impact all this incredible content (or saying and showing what others aren't willing to say) has had on Greg's company, here's one of the thousands of comments on their YouTube channel:

> *"Checked out all your reviews with the Herman Miller and Steelcase chairs. Out of all of them, the Mirra 2 was the most adjustable and it ticked all the boxes for me. I wanted an all-mesh chair so I tried out an Aeron and Mirra 2 in a local used office furniture place and fell in love with the Mirra 2's arms and rocking chair motion. Ended up buying the fully loaded Mirra 2 with the Butterfly back as the foam/mesh made the back super comfortable. My butt and back thanks your in-depth reviews!"*

9 | Topic 5: Best in Class

The final topic of The Big 5 is "Best" or "Best in Class."

Think about how often you've gone online and searched for a phrase like "Best (product/company)" or "Best (type of business) in (location)."

It's practically second nature, isn't it? But when it comes to these "best"-related searches, the word "best" is just one of many descriptors we use as buyers to "rank" or "classify" what we're researching.

Here are some of the other common phrases buyers use to explore options and make comparisons:

- Most / Least
- Best / Worst
- Highest / Lowest
- Fastest / Slowest
- Strongest / Weakest
- Loudest / Quietest
- Biggest / Smallest
- Newest / Oldest
- Safest / Riskiest
- Brightest / Dimmest
- Heaviest / Lightest
- Thickest / Thinnest

- Richest / Poorest
- Easiest / Hardest
- Cleanest / Dirtiest
- Cheapest / Most Expensive
- Quickest / Longest
- Smartest / Dumbest
- Warmest / Coldest
- Sharpest / Dullest

As you review this list, think about the products or services you offer. How many of your potential customers are searching with these terms to guide their decision-making?

Remember Steven Sheinkopf from Yale Appliance, whom we met in the introduction? His experience with the "Least Serviced, Most Reliable Appliance Brands" is a classic example of best-in-class content, which is why his article and video series have been so successful.

Best (Company) Near Me

There are countless ways consumers use "best" and similar phrases in searches, but one of the most common habits we've all developed is typing "Best (type of company) in (location)" or "Best (type of company) near me."

Take, for instance, a story from my early days as a pool guy starting out with They Ask, You Answer. I recall a sales appointment in Richmond, Virginia, where, after spending almost three hours with a couple, going over every detail and giving them a quote, they said to me, "Marcus, we like you. We're pretty sure we want to get this pool from you. But if we didn't, is there anyone else you'd recommend?"

I was bummed—obviously, they were still shopping around. And I didn't close the sale that night.

On the long drive home, though, I reflected on their question. They had essentially asked, "Who are the best pool builders in Richmond, Virginia?" And then it hit me—why not answer that question online myself?

That evening, I went home and wrote an article for our website titled, "Who Are the Best Pool Builders in Richmond, Virginia (Reviews/Ratings)." In that article, I listed five of the best pool builders in Richmond.

And how did I choose the five?

That was easy. They were the companies I'd lost the most deals to over the years.

When I shared this article idea with my two business partners, they were concerned about being that transparent. I was talking openly about competitors—something no pool company had ever done before. My message to them was simple: There are no secrets here. If potential customers want information on our competitors, they're going to get it somehow. Why shouldn't they get it from us?

For transparency's sake, I didn't even include our company on the list, because I wanted to avoid appearing biased.

And what was the result? That article has since generated more than $1 million in revenue for our company in Virginia. Not only did it rank for the phrase "Best Pool Builders Richmond Virginia," but it also ranked for several of our competitors' keywords.

In fact, I once had a customer tell me, "Marcus, I was about to sign a contract with one of your competitors, but as I researched them, I stumbled across your article. I thought, 'Wow, these guys are so honest—I should probably call them too.'"

That lady bought a pool from us. All because we dared to address a question no one else would.

That's the power of transparency.

That's the power of saying what no one else is willing to say.

One Final Note on Best-in-Class Content

In *They Ask, You Answer* and for years, we've advised companies not to include themselves on "Best of" lists. The reason is simple: If the content is worded incorrectly, it can come across as biased and self-serving, risking a loss of trust.

But AI is changing our perspective on this advice. These "best of" lists are increasingly what AI models are drawing from to make recommendations. This introduces a new balancing act where we need to "train" and "teach" AI while avoiding the appearance of self-promotion and bias.

The takeaway? Use your best judgment. No matter how you approach it, "best" content is here to stay, and you need to be part of the conversation.

Reader's Resources: Check out the EC Companion Guide for more examples of exceptional Big 5 content, proven tips to get your team started, and tools to make your content creation process easier and more effective.

10 | Getting Started with The Big 5

Feeling inspired by The Big 5? Overflowing with content ideas your company needs to create?

Perfect.

That's the mindset of a business ready to transform.

In this chapter, we'll map out the practical steps you'll take to bring The Big 5 to life, building trust with your audience and paving the way for remarkable growth.

Start with a Content Brainstorm—And Use AI to Do It

If you commit to the Endless Customers journey, you'll hold your first brainstorming session to generate Big 5 content ideas as part of your kick-off, which we call **Alignment Day.** This all-day session is when your entire team—leadership, sales, marketing, service delivery, and customer service—comes together to align on the Endless Customers initiative as a whole.

During this session, you'll draw on the insights of everyone who interacts with your customers to identify the most pressing questions and concerns your buyers have. We'll talk more about what Alignment Day entails in the final section, "Putting It All Together."

In the early days of *They Ask, You Answer*, marketing teams relied solely on brainstorming sessions like this to generate content ideas.

But the game has changed.

Today, you can utilize AI to enhance and accelerate your Big 5 content efforts. AI tools can help identify patterns, surface additional questions, and generate ideas that complement the insights from your team.

So whether you're just starting on your Endless Customers journey or you've been practicing its principles for years, AI is your ally in creating and refining Big 5 content. However, to get the highest-quality outputs, you need to teach the AI about your business.

Here's how to start:

1. **Train your AI on The Big 5.** To help AI generate valuable Big 5 content, you first need to teach it the basics. Don't worry—this part is easy. You can find a prewritten AI prompt in the EC Companion Guide that is designed to train your AI tool on the fundamentals of The Big 5.

2. **Feed the AI real business data.** Provide your AI tool with real inputs like sales call transcripts, marketing collateral, website content, and FAQs. The more relevant and detailed the information, the better the AI's understanding and suggestions will be.

3. **Compile ideas for The Big 5 topics.** Use the AI to generate lists of questions and ideas for each Big 5 topic across your core products, services, or solutions.

4. **Vet the ideas with your team.** Share the AI-generated list with your sales and customer service teams. They can help refine the ideas, identify gaps, and ensure the content aligns with the real questions and concerns your buyers are expressing.

Focus on Your Core Product or Service First

With an open sea of content opportunities, it can be hard to figure out where to start.

My advice? Start with what you're trying to sell the most.

What's the bread and butter of your business? For most companies, there's usually one or two core offerings that drive the majority of revenue. This is where you need to focus your efforts at the beginning.

Within that focus, I generally recommend starting with **cost and price content first.**

Why? Because it's often the most immediately helpful for your sales team to use in the sales process. Buyers consistently want to know what a product or service will cost, and addressing this question early helps build trust and remove barriers to purchase.

Once your major cost and price pieces are complete, you can move on to other Big 5 content for your primary product or service.

From there, you can expand to cover additional products or services, ensuring you build a comprehensive library of content that serves your buyers' needs at every stage of their journey.

> **Reader's Resources:** Grab your copy of our pre-written AI prompt and get a head start on training your AI tool on the fundamentals of The Big 5. While you're there, check out tons of examples of standout Big 5 content to spark ideas.

Create Your Content

Once you have a vetted list and focus, it's time to get to work. AI can assist you here, too:

1. **Draft content.** Use AI to outline or draft initial versions of your articles, videos, or podcasts.
2. **Pull in real data.** Marketing teams can supplement AI drafts by pulling details from sales call recordings or interviewing sales team members.
3. **Always use human oversight.** AI can be a powerful tool, but it should not replace the human element in content creation. Human oversight is mandatory to ensure content aligns with your brand's voice, maintains authenticity, and builds trust.

Remember: AI should *never* be your sole content creator. We'll dive deeper into the importance of human intervention in Section 5, "Be More Human."

> **Reader's Resources:** Need an extra set of eyes on your Big 5 content? We've got you covered. Go to the EC Companion Guide to access our custom-built Endless Customers Content Reviewer. Simply paste your draft into the reviewer to receive actionable feedback, including tips for improvement.
>
>

Build a Backlog of Content, Publish, and Never Stop

Before you start publishing, aim to build a backlog of 5–10 pieces of content. This ensures consistency in your publishing schedule and allows for flexibility if unexpected delays arise. Consistency isn't just rewarded by algorithms—it's necessary to build a strong audience.

Once your backlog is ready, **start publishing at least three new pieces of Big 5 content every week**. Don't let perfection hold you back. Publish now; tweak and improve as you go. Perfection is the enemy of progress.

Finally, this is a marathon, not a sprint. Publishing consistent, high-quality Big 5 content will help you build trust, dominate your niche, and become the most known and trusted brand in your space.

Expand to Other Mediums

While much of The Big 5 has traditionally been considered the written word, we're actually talking about *all* content formats. Think bigger than just a blog post or page on your website—this content should be present on your social platforms, YouTube channel, newsletter, podcast, and more.

If you start with written content, repurpose it into video or audio formats to reach buyers in their preferred learning style. For example, create a YouTube video or podcast episode based on an article you've already published, then embed the video into the original article to enhance its reach and utility.

Video, in particular, is becoming increasingly valuable as AI-generated search results pull written content directly into results pages without requiring users to click through. Video offers an opportunity to stand out, rank highly, and engage buyers directly on platforms like YouTube.

And speaking of video, in Section 3 we'll discuss the second pillar on how to effectively show your audience what others in your space aren't willing to show them.

Show What Others Aren't Willing to Show

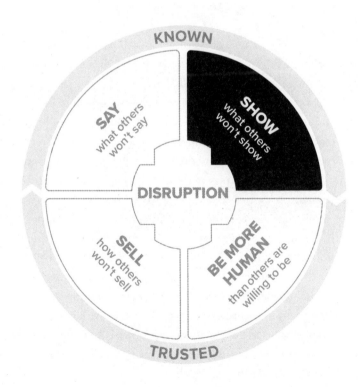

Video is transforming the world as we know it.

Businesses that use it effectively are experiencing incredible growth, and those that continue to ignore its power and potential are being left behind. And this trend isn't going to slow down anytime soon.

As humans, we don't want to just read about something. We want to *see* it. Because if we can see it, we feel that we can verify it. And if it's verified, it must be true.

In other words, video is fundamentally about becoming more known and driving trust—the core purpose of Endless Customers. Which brings us to the second pillar of becoming a known and trusted brand: **Show what others aren't willing to show**.

Take a moment to reflect on how much your business currently reveals through video that the majority of your industry and competitors are hesitant to share. It's one thing to have a few videos on your website. It's another to create videos that make viewers say, "I had no idea that's how it worked," or "Wow, now I get it," or "I feel like I already know you from watching your video."

Let's look at an example of a company willing to be bold enough to show what no one else is willing to show, from Opes Partners, a property investment company based in New Zealand.

Most organizations don't want to show how they select their suppliers, the types of questions they ask, and what they value—mainly because most are afraid that someone else (a competitor) will "steal their secret sauce."

But Opes Partners threw that concern out the window with their You-Tube show *The Deal*, which took potential suppliers—real estate developers who build rental properties that Opes Partners sells to its investors—and had them pitch new developments for inclusion into the Opes Partners portfolio. In essence, these developers were being grilled for the ability to put their product in front of their clients.

Without these suppliers, Opes Partners has no product for their investors, and yet they grilled these folks. They asked incredibly hard questions, all of it on video, and then presented it just like you would see on the popular American business reality television series *Shark Tank*. This showed their future investors exactly how detailed the team is and how each property investment is vetted—thus revealing their secret sauce.

On top of it all, it was incredibly entertaining to watch.

Where did this take them? After amassing a large audience on their YouTube channel, Opes Partners evolved *The Deal* into what has now become the most listened-to business podcast in all of New Zealand—*The Property Academy Podcast.*

The lesson is clear: You need to start showing what others in your space aren't willing to show.

No matter the industry, there's a massive gap between what businesses are claiming and what they're actually showing.

And the ones willing to bridge that gap? They're the ones who will stand out.

In this section, we're going to challenge the way you see and use video within your organization. You'll discover the seven types of videos that have the greatest impact on your sales team—The Selling 7. You'll also learn powerful frameworks to elevate the way you create and leverage video on YouTube, social media, and your website.

And finally, we'll showcase a few examples of companies that are truly "showing what no one else is willing to show."

11 | The Future of Video and Becoming a "Media Company"

Take a moment and consider how much video you consume in a day.

Now, compare that to just a few years ago.

Think about your daily routine. You're scrolling through social media, watching shorts and stories on your phone. You're clicking through videos while researching products or seeking answers to questions. Your inbox and messages are filled with video links from colleagues, friends, and family.

Sure, you might be one of the rare few who says, "I don't watch videos." That's fine—but look around.

Everyone else is watching more than ever before.

The numbers tell the story: Video now accounts for over 82% of all internet traffic.

Let that sink in.

And this isn't just a trend—it's a tidal wave that's only gaining momentum. Where will we be in 5–10 years? It's almost impossible to imagine.

But one thing is crystal clear: **The age of video isn't just here—it's taking over.**

Becoming a "Media Company"

This shift puts immense pressure on companies and organizations not just to be good with video, but to be *great at it*.

And how do you become great? The first step is deciding whether video is a true priority—agreeing, as a team, that video is of monumental importance to becoming a known and trusted brand. Once this has been agreed upon, the next step is having the right mindset.

What's the right mindset? It's that of a **media company**.

Yes, a *media* company.

If your organization is going to become great with video, you must start to see your business exactly like a media company would.

I experienced this mindset shift a couple of years into doing They Ask, You Answer with my swimming pool company. I could see where the world was heading in terms of video and realized that no longer could we be passive when it came to "showing" what customers wanted to know. The way we viewed ourselves shifted dramatically during this time period, evolving from "We're a fiberglass swimming pool company" to "We're a media company that brings families together by showing (through video) the positive impact of swimming pools on our lives."

Once we made this shift, our strategic vision of video went from "What types of videos should we be creating?" to "Everything we do as a company, everything we sell, and everything we install is a story to be told. We just need to show it."

Can you see the difference?

This is a hard mindset to develop and ingratiate across an organization, but once it happens, magic comes with it.

Later in the book, we'll explore what it means to operate like a media company internally—tailored, of course, to the size of your organization. For now, it's important to understand that mindset is the key to harnessing the power of video. Unless your company takes it seriously, you'll never fully realize how impactful, disruptive, and transformative it can be for your business.

Overcoming Personal Biases with Video

And one more thing about "mindset" before we dive into the rest of this section on video and showing what others aren't willing to show.

As you read through this section of the book, you may find yourself thinking about any or all of the following:

> *"I don't really watch much video; it's just not my thing."*
> *"We don't see much video in our niche."*
> *"I'm just not good on video."*

While these feelings may be valid, decades of business experience have taught me one hard truth: **We can't let personal opinions interfere with smart business decisions.**

The good thing is that many companies out there have gotten past their biases and have done some extraordinary things with video. In fact, everything you read in this section has been proven to work with the hundreds of clients we've helped at IMPACT to create a culture of video and become a literal media company.

This is why you must remember this: **Getting into business means committing to meet the market where it is.**

And where is the market today? It's with video.

Video is what consumers and buyers want, and it's how they want to learn. If you want to be seen by your market as the most known and trusted brand, you can't afford to be passive with video. You need to think like a media company and show what others in your space aren't willing to show.

Now, let's explore exactly how you can make that happen.

12

Videos That Move the Sales Needle: The Selling 7

For the last decade, my team at IMPACT has been teaching organizations how to think like media companies, helping them to create videos that *actually* move the needle for sales and marketing. These videos aren't just nice-to-have assets or fluff pieces; they're strategic tools designed to drive revenue.

When companies follow our guidance and have a solid video strategy—producing the *right* videos, sharing them on the *right* platforms, and using them strategically in both sales and marketing—they see results.

Big results.

Shorter sales cycles.

More informed prospects.

Faster deal closures.

That's what happens when you get this right.

What we've found is that all too often, businesses venture into video production blindly. They pour time and money into video production, only to get little to no return on investment. And they're frustrated. Why? Because they're doing it wrong.

It's not enough to just *make videos*—you've got to make the *right videos* and use them in the *right way*. If you're not doing that, video won't deliver the results you're after. And that's not because video doesn't work—it's because you're not working it right.

To address this common challenge, we developed seven types of videos that provide a powerful boost to sales and marketing, especially when effectively utilized by the sales team. We call these videos **The Selling 7.**

The Selling 7

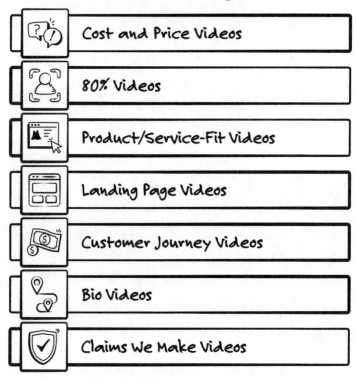

Cost and Price Videos

80% Videos

Product/Service-Fit Videos

Landing Page Videos

Customer Journey Videos

Bio Videos

Claims We Make Videos

1. **Cost and Price Videos:** Here, we take what we learned from The Big 5 a step further, and bring it to life in video. You're *showing* your audience not just *what* drives price but *why,* and increasing its effectiveness visually.

2. **The 80% Video:** Eighty percent of the questions your sales team gets asked are the same. This type of video addresses those frequently asked questions head-on, preparing prospects before they ever speak with your team, saving everyone time.

3. **Product/Service-Fit Videos:** Buyers want to see what they're getting. These videos showcase your products or services in action, highlighting their features, benefits, and what makes them unique.

4. **Landing Page Videos:** First impressions matter. Adding a short, engaging video to your landing pages can instantly increase conversions by helping visitors quickly understand why your offer matters and why they should take action.

5. **Customer Journey Videos:** Nothing builds trust like seeing how others have succeeded with your business. These videos tell the story of your customers' experiences, showcasing real results and humanizing your brand.

6. **Bio Videos:** People buy from people they trust. Bio videos introduce your team in a personal, approachable way, making your sales team relatable and creating connections before the first handshake—virtual or otherwise.

7. **The Claims We Make Videos:** Every company makes claims, but not all back them up. These videos tackle the claims you make about your business, showing buyers how you deliver on your promises with clear evidence and examples.

These seven types of videos are directly tied to the questions and concerns we explored in The Big 5, making them familiar and, at first glance, deceptively simple. You might think, "Great, I'll just whip up a quick video on cost or throw together a product demo." But here's the thing: Simplicity doesn't mean easy.

For these videos to actually deliver results—whether that's shorter sales cycles, more qualified leads, or faster deal closures—they need to be done right. That means understanding not just *what* to say, but *how* to say it, *where* to use it, and *when* it will have the greatest impact.

So let's unpack each type of video to dive deeper into what makes it effective and how you can leverage it to transform your business.

Video 1: Cost and Price Videos

The first step in your journey with The Selling 7 is to create a detailed video dedicated to discussing the cost and price of the product or service you offer. Just as your written content should begin at the decision-making stage of the buyer's journey, so should your video strategy.

One of the most powerful advantages of using video in the sales process is that it allows salespeople to clearly communicate the cost and value of a product or service—even when they aren't there in person. Instead of relying on a secondhand explanation from a messenger to other decision-makers, you can share a video that conveys the value of your product in your own words, exactly as intended.

A great Cost and Price Video, similar to what was stated when we discussed cost within the context of The Big 5, should specifically:

- Address all the factors that influence the cost of a product or service.
- Discuss the marketplace—why similar products, services, or companies may vary in price, whether cheap, expensive, or otherwise.
- Explain why your product or service costs what it does, clearly conveying your value proposition.

To be effective, each video should focus on only one specific product or service. If you offer multiple main products or services, you'll want to create a separate price/cost video for each.

Make the videos as long as necessary to thoroughly answer the question. In most cases, we find these videos run from five to eight minutes, though there are certainly instances where shorter or longer videos may be appropriate, depending on the subject matter.

Video 2: The 80% Video

We've been training sales teams around the globe for more than a decade, and whenever we ask them—regardless of industry—what percentage of questions they receive on sales calls are essentially the same, the answer is almost always between 70 and 90%.

Enter the 80% Video.

The 80% Video addresses the most common questions your prospects ask during the sales process, particularly the ones your sales team wishes buyers already understood. This video enables prospects to move more quickly through the buyer's journey, allowing sales conversations to focus on the client's unique needs rather than revisiting the standard FAQs. This shift not only builds trust but also accelerates the sales process in a positive way for both sides.

The key to this type of video, though, is to concentrate not just on what you want the buyer to know, but on the questions you know are most pressing for them.

As with the cost and price video, you'll want to create one 80% Video for each major product or service you offer.

When used correctly, this video has an incredible impact on moving the sales needle. Later, in Section 4, "Sell How Others Aren't Willing to Sell," we'll discuss how to leverage the 80% Video more effectively within the sales process.

Video 3: Product/Service-Fit Videos

There's no faster way to communicate the value proposition of a specific product or service than through video.

On the product and service pages of your website, you should address most of the key questions buyers have during the buying process. Each of these pages should include a video, typically under five minutes, that helps answer the question "But is it right for me?"

Creating this type of video successfully depends on following the Law of the Coin: You must be genuine and upfront about both sides of the "good-fit" and "bad-fit" conversation. Many companies claim to have great Product/Service-Fit Videos, but too often, they've simply made pitch videos that focus only on the positives. A true Product/Service-Fit Video should be balanced, addressing both the advantages and limitations, to ensure it resonates with the right buyers.

Video 4: Landing Page Videos

When someone is prompted to fill out a form on your website, like the "Contact Us" page, they usually have four primary concerns:

1. Will this company spam me if I provide my email?
2. If I give them my phone number, are they going to keep calling me?
3. Privacy concerns: What are they going to do with my personal information?
4. What exactly happens next if I complete this form?

Understanding that these are the common concerns, you can address them directly by adding a video titled "See Exactly What Will Happen if You Fill Out This Form" next to the form itself.

Wondering what to say in this video? Here's an example script:

> *"Alright, you might be sitting there thinking, 'Should I really fill out this form? Are they going to spam me or call me repeatedly? And what exactly are they going to do with my information?' If you're asking yourself these questions, don't worry! Here's exactly what will happen (and what won't) once you fill out this form."*

Don't underestimate the power of Landing Page Videos. Our clients have seen remarkable results. In fact, most companies experience a conversion lift for that form in the range of 80%, nearly doubling the number of people filling it out.

Video 5: Customer Journey Videos

As we've discussed, social proof and reviews are essential in today's buying process. While most companies include general text testimonials on their site, the most impactful form of social proof is what we call Customer Journey Videos.

If you've ever watched an infomercial, you already have a sense of what a Customer Journey Video should convey. Ideally, much like "The Hero's Journey" in every Disney movie, a Customer Journey Video should illustrate the three key stages of a buyer's journey with your company:

1. The problem, need, or concern they were trying to solve.
2. How they discovered your company and the journey they went on with your team (in storytelling terms, you play the "guide").
3. The impact of buying from you on their life, organization, or situation.

When used effectively—on social media, your website, and within your sales process—these videos resonate with potential customers, prompting them to think, "They've worked with someone just like me." This response is exactly what you're aiming for, because it signifies that you're building immediate and meaningful trust.

Video 6: Bio Videos

One of the biggest reasons why video is such a powerful tool is that it allows your prospects to see, hear, and get to know you before they actually meet you. This is especially true with an employee's Bio Video—a simple yet powerful tool that everyone on your sales team should be utilizing.

Bio Videos are exactly what they sound like: short videos where your team members speak directly to the camera and introduce themselves. Generally, you want to cover two main points in these videos:

1. What they do in their role and why they love it.
2. A bit about themselves on a personal level.

Once these videos are created for each salesperson, embed them in their email signatures, along with their name, contact information, and photo.

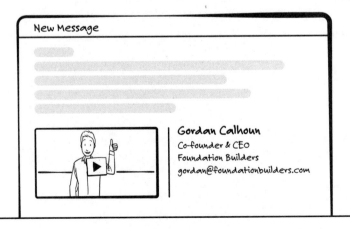

Creating these types of videos is a classic example of showcasing a more human side of your company—one that most competitors won't match.

Video 7: The Claims We Make Video

Think about how many claims your organization makes. Some of the most common include statements like:

> *"It's our people that make us different."*
> *"Our customer service is second to none."*
> *"We have the best guarantee in the industry."*

The issue with claims like these is that everyone makes them. Over time, they become little more than background noise to your audience.

To stand out, start by listing all the claims you make as a company, especially those used in the sales process. Then ask yourself, "How many of these claims have we proven to be true with video?"

Once you have your list, find ways to "show" each claim with video, demonstrating why it's true. Doing this will be yet another powerful example of showing what your competitors aren't willing to show.

With the Claims We Make Videos, we round out The Selling 7—a lineup of videos that have consistently proven their ability to drive increased brand awareness, trust, leads, and sales.

Creating these videos—especially if you sell multiple products or services—will keep one videographer busy for months. Once you consider all the pre- and post-production, as well as the ongoing creation of new videos, you'll see that the job never stops. We'll discuss this in detail later in the book when we take a look at the role and duties of a full-time in-house videographer. Such a role may seem intimidating and expensive now, but they will be one of the greatest investments your company will ever make.

13 | YouTube's Importance for Endless Customers

YouTube's significance in your organization's ability to become the most known and trusted brand in your market cannot be overstated. Why? Because as AI platforms like ChatGPT lessen Google's dominance on search—hurting website traffic across the board—companies need to counter these losses by leaning much more into YouTube and social media platforms as well.

Some may consider YouTube to be a social media platform, but we argue that it's actually much more a search engine for video content, as well as a general entertainment/education media platform. Here's why: For more than a decade, YouTube has been a dominant force in the search engine world, second only to Google. Many of those searches are buying-related, with millions of users turning to YouTube for tutorials, product demos, and insights.

YouTube: The Search Engine You're Overlooking

YouTube isn't just big—it's where buyers go to find answers.

In fact, various studies suggest that more than 70% of people, including your customers, use YouTube to solve problems they're experiencing at work or in their lives. They also evaluate products or services on YouTube before making purchasing decisions. This number, just as all the others we've mentioned in the book, is only increasing with time.

Google also favors YouTube videos. Their algorithms prioritize the content that best answers their users' questions, and in their eyes—and in ours—video does that best. Of the video results they show, an estimated 80% come from YouTube, which isn't surprising, considering Google owns YouTube. Search anything on Google related to a topic included in The Big 5, and you'll likely see YouTube videos at the top.

Why does this matter? Because YouTube presents one of the most effective paths to getting found in Google search results today. Studies suggest that videos, particularly YouTube videos, are far more likely to appear in Google search results compared to traditional content, with some estimates suggesting a 50-fold advantage. Plus, videos also tend to achieve higher click-through rates, making them a powerful tool for engagement.

Why YouTube Is About More Than SEO

It's tempting to think of YouTube primarily as an SEO tool—and it absolutely is. But its value goes deeper than that. Unlike a single blog post, a well-optimized YouTube channel is a living, breathing library of resources that works for you 24/7. Every tutorial, product demo, customer testimonial, or educational video you post becomes another point of connection with your audience.

As we discuss the types of videos you need to create in this chapter, keep in mind the majority should go on your company's YouTube page.

Furthermore, you should value your YouTube page just as you would your website, because its impact on your business and ability to become more known and trusted will only grow with time.

How to Treat YouTube Like Your Website

If you're serious about building an audience of endless customers, your YouTube channel needs to be more than a dumping ground for random videos. It should be treated with the same level of care, strategy, and consistency as your website. That means:

1. **Optimizing your channel:** Create playlists for key topics, use descriptive titles and tags, and ensure your branding is consistent.
2. **Posting regularly:** A dead channel doesn't inspire trust. Commit to publishing content consistently, even if it's just one video a week.
3. **Focusing on quality:** Your videos don't need to be Hollywood productions, but they should be clear, engaging, and professional.
4. **Driving action:** Include strong calls to action (CTAs) in every video, whether it's subscribing to your channel, visiting your website, or contacting your sales team.

The ultimate goal of Endless Customers is to make your brand the most known and trusted voice in your industry. YouTube accelerates that process in dramatic ways. It gives you visibility, builds credibility, and provides a platform to answer the questions your buyers are already asking.

Reader's Resources: To learn about the many other best practices to building an extraordinary YouTube channel and presence, refer to the EC Companion Guide.

Produce Episodic Content to Repurpose Across Different Channels

To truly maximize the impact of your video strategy, consistency, and planning are key. One approach that has proven highly effective is creating episodic content—structured video series that keep audiences engaged and coming back for more.

Episodic content isn't just about creating videos; it's about building a recognizable series that fosters trust and anticipation. By designing content that follows a predictable format or schedule, you create opportunities for repurposing it across multiple platforms, such as YouTube, podcasts, and social media. This not only broadens your reach, but it also reinforces your brand's authority and keeps your audience engaged.

When creating episodic content, especially for platforms like YouTube, blend video and audio formats where possible. Using the framework of The Big 5, you can create episodes that not only educate but entertain.

With advancements in AI, repurposing content has never been easier. Today, there's technology that can turn your written content into audio versions, automatically distribute it, and even optimize it for different platforms.

As with all things, there's a caveat: Will this approach elicit trust? Will it set you apart, or will it push you back into the sea of sameness?

While AI tools can streamline production, it's important to ensure that your content remains personal, engaging, and genuinely valuable.

Consider the *Endless Customers* podcast. What started as a podcast is now so much more—it's a YouTube show, a content driver for social posts, an asset for our newsletter, and an integral part of our overall content calendar. Every episode feeds multiple channels, ensuring that the content we create is accessible and valuable no matter how our audience prefers to consume it.

Now that we've highlighted the importance of using video to build trust and expand your reach, it's time to explore proven ways to make your videos more engaging.

14

The Structure for Videos That Capture and Excite

Think back to the last time you started watching a video. Maybe it was a tutorial, a product review, or even an explainer video. What made you stay? Better yet, why did you *stop* watching and click away? Was the video slow to get to the point? Did it feel irrelevant? Or maybe it just didn't grab you in those crucial first few seconds?

In today's fast-paced, click-happy world, capturing someone's initial attention isn't enough—you must also work to *keep* your audience engaged. And whether you're creating content to educate, entertain, or convert, the success of your video comes down to structure. Without a clear plan, even the best ideas fall flat.

That's why I developed a proven method to structure your videos—one that hooks viewers immediately, keeps them engaged, and leaves them inspired to take action. In this chapter, I'll walk you through the exact framework we've used with hundreds of businesses to create videos that *excite* their audience and deliver results.

Let's dive into two powerful tools: **The QQPP Method** for crafting irresistible introductions, and **The Video 6,** a repeatable structure that transforms your long-form videos into compelling, high-retention content.

For Long-Form Videos: The Video 6

Ever wish you had the perfect way to start a video or article that hooks your audience every time? Or maybe you've wondered how to keep viewers from clicking away within those vital first few seconds?

Because attention and retention are so essential with all online content these days, I developed a simple method that anyone can follow to start any piece of content—video, article, or audio.

It's called **The QQPP Method,** which stands for Question, Question, Promise, Preview. It is an incredibly simple way you can start your videos while drawing in your audience and giving them a clear reason to stay with your content until the end.

There are two distinct parts to a great intro using QQPP: the questions and the promise/preview.

In part one, the goal is to make the viewer quickly nod their head—using their very own questions, concerns, or worries to help them immediately realize they have found the right piece of content to answer or address something that is specific to them.

For example, let's say you're a company looking to embrace the Endless Customers System and our coaching team at IMPACT wanted to create a video to speak to you. It might start this way:

> *Have you recently read* Endless Customers *and felt like you'd like to apply it to your business? Looking for a company that can train you on the Endless Customers methodology and hold your hand through the entire process?*

Notice how each of these questions basically rewords the exact same need or question. In this case, they are designed to make someone who has read *Endless Customers* feel they've come to the perfect place to find the help/guidance they're looking for. In fact, if you do the "QQ" part of this method correctly, many of your readers or viewers will literally nod their heads, as if to say, "Yes, that's me!"

Next, we move to the second part, the promise/preview of the opening dialogue. When it comes to promise/preview, the goal is simple: Tell them what you're going to discuss in the video, and tell them what the payoff will be in the end, or what they'll walk away with.

Continuing with the earlier example, we would likely say something like:

> *"Well, if you are looking for help and guidance to apply Endless Customers, this video was made for you. In it, we'll look at the different types of coaching we offer, we'll explain who is and who is not a good fit for each, and by the end, you'll know whether Endless Customers coaching is right for you."*

The promise here is that they will get a clear sense about whether coaching is a fit for their needs. The preview comes in mentioning how we'll discuss the types of coaching offered, as well as who is or isn't a good fit for the program.

Here's a fill-in-the-blank script you can use for QQPP:

Are you wondering _____?

Do you _____?

If so, you're in the right place.

In this video, you'll learn _____.

By the end, you'll be able to decide _____.

This method can be applied to any piece of content you create. Once you've done it a few times, you'll find it becomes simple and natural to use this opening structure in all your content. In other words, you'll never again get stuck overthinking the question "How do I start?" every time you create a new piece of content.

Once you've learned The QQPP Method, the next step with your longer-form videos is to follow what we call **The Video 6**—a powerful method to structure your videos to increase views and retention while also creating a better viewing experience.

The Video Six

1. **The Teaser:** The teaser is the first 10–30 seconds of your video. This is your hook, where you capture the viewer's attention. It doesn't matter how great your content is if you can't get viewers past those first few seconds. Make it compelling, and give them a reason to stick around. This is a great place to use your QQPP Method introduction.

2. **The Logo Bumper:** A logo bumper is a short motion graphic that includes your company logo, branding your video and setting the tone. These days, it's quite easy to create a logo bumper using simple and inexpensive tools or with the help of AI. Don't overthink it—just make a quick bumper (a few seconds is plenty) that can be reused with each long-form video you produce.

   Keep in mind, though, that we do not recommend logo bumpers on your short-form, vertical videos, or really any video under 60 seconds, because they will only hurt retention rates and, ultimately, view counts. Stick to using this in your long-form video only.

3. **The Intro:** This is where you or the subject of the video introduces themself and the content. While the teaser quickly grabs attention and does a degree of introducing the topic, the full introduction elaborates on what the video is about. This is where you set expectations and explain why the content is important. Use this time to get buy-in from your audience and preview what's coming in the segments to follow.

4. **Segments:** Have you ever watched a long video with no breaks? You probably started zoning out, thinking about lunch, or looking at suggested videos. Segments break up the content into manageable chunks, improving viewer retention and recollection. Think of segmenting like subheaders on an online article—something that is key to providing order for the brain as well as a sense of progress.

   For a video, the beginning of each segment often has a title card or some sort of visual overlay that labels or introduces the next segment. So whether it's five steps or a how-to guide, segmenting helps your audience digest information and stay engaged.

5. **The Call-to-Action (CTA):** A good marketing and sales video always has a CTA. After arming your viewers with information, what's the next best step they should take? Be specific about what they should do next and why. Use visual cues to show what that next step looks like, whether it's visiting a webpage, watching another video, or downloading a resource.

   Just be sure to always plan your CTA *before* you shoot the video. This way, it's intentional, thoughtful, and as effective as possible.

6. **The Outro:** The outro is your final chance to leave your viewer with a positive feeling while bringing it all together. Make it count. Generally, one of the best ways to do this is to quickly summarize what you've told them, call back your original promise, and give them some type of charge or action step as they look ahead.

Of course, there are other structures you can use with your long-form video content, but when it comes to a repeatable method that will help your team consistently produce helpful, engaging, and effective video, especially when it comes to The Big 5 and The Selling 7, this is a great place to start.

15

The Power of Vertical Video on Social Media

Vertical, short-form videos (we'll just call them short-form video from now on) are taking over, and businesses need to pay attention.

This is no exaggeration—**People are obsessed with short-form videos.**

In fact, the average person watches over an hour of short-form video a day, a stunning number considering they are still rather new to the market.

For those unfamiliar with what I mean by the term "short-form video," I'm specifically talking about videos like the ones you see as YouTube Shorts, Facebook and Instagram Reels, and TikToks. Short-form videos are filmed and produced vertically, tailored for mobile devices, and, as the name implies, are short, usually just 5–90 seconds long on average (although this is constantly evolving, depending on the platform).

The stats and studies both prove the market's preference for shorter video content, with short-form videos receiving two and a half times the amount of engagement—clicks, comments, shares, and other types of engagement—compared to long-form videos.[1]

In 2016, TikTok's "vertical-only" videos revolutionized the market, leading to a significant shift in video consumption habits. These videos, combined with a perfect algorithm, engaged viewers in a way that's similar to the dopamine rush of a slot machine, keeping them coming back for more. This sparked a dramatic shift in user behavior, forcing platforms like YouTube, Facebook, and Instagram to follow suit with their own short, vertical video features as they scrambled to catch up with where social media users were directing their attention.

While there are slight differences between these platforms, they share a common essence of brief, engaging content designed for mobile-first consumption. Content that performs well on one of these platforms often translates effectively to others.

Beyond entertainment, short-form video has also fueled the rise of microlearning—engaging lessons on a topic delivered in just a few minutes, which has become a significant trend moving forward.

While we could debate how healthy these short-form, vertical videos are for the world, no one can deny their extreme impact on the minds and behavior of all consumers. Remember, as businesses, we must not allow personal opinions—such as whether or not we like video, YouTube, or TikTok—to prevent us from making smart business decisions.

If your market is consuming this type of content (and they likely are), you need to be producing it. It's about meeting your customers where they are. Think about how you can bring your content about The Big 5 to short-form video. For example, people flipping through short-form videos love to watch comparison content. How can you get creative with your comparison content, using video to really show the differences? Could you explain what something costs in less than 90 seconds effectively? Of course you could.

But keep this in mind when it comes to short-form versus long-form video: Generally, short-form is much more about awareness of a brand. If you want to make the largest possible number of people aware of your brand, then short-form is likely a smart place to start. On the other hand, if you're looking to educate or entertain an existing audience, generally long-form is the route to go.

And just like with YouTube, buyers are discovering products or services through short-form video while connecting with the people behind the products, such as the creators, influencers, or even the businesses themselves. This kind of personal connection goes a long way in building trust, and trust turns viewers into buyers.

With this being said, the key to effective short-form video comes down to one simple catchphrase: **"Make them click. Make them stick."**

In other words, you want to give viewers a strong reason to click on your video and then stay until the end. Driving retention dramatically increases your chance of getting more views, which in turn helps your brand become more known and trusted.

Make Them Click and Make Them Stick with The Sticky 5

Remember, the name of the game with short-form video is to grab their attention and hold that attention all the way to the end of the video. Typically, the higher your click-through rate and retention rate are on a video, the more YouTube or other social media platforms will want to show it.

For this reason, I've developed a simple method anyone can follow to give you the best chance at retaining more viewership throughout the video and increasing your chances of virality. I call it **The Sticky 5** and here's what it includes:

The Sticky Five of Vertical Video

1. The Hook
2. Three-Second Rule
3. Progress Principle
4. Payoff Principle
5. Quit While You're Ahead Principle

1. **The Hook:** The title of the video, as well as the first few seconds, must really "hook" the viewer and give them a reason to stay. Whether it's curiosity, intrigue, or surprise—don't waste a second (literally) on any fluff. Draw them in immediately, but make sure your hook relates to the first frame of the video they'll see when scrolling. Otherwise, they may be disappointed and quickly move on. But the key here is establishing a curiosity gap from the second they see the title to literally the end of the video.

2. **The 3-Second Rule:** Once you've grabbed a viewer's attention with the initial hook, it's time to keep their interest. One of the biggest keys to this is what we refer to as The 3-Second Rule, which essentially means you ideally want a "cut" in your video every three seconds. In other words, things should feel like they are constantly changing—a different angle or a new shot—anything that makes the video feel like it's moving quickly is key here.

   While it may not always be possible to have a cut or new scene every three seconds, getting close to this cadence can significantly improve your retention rates, which is the ultimate goal. By maintaining this rhythm, you can tell a "long" story in a very short period of time, keeping your viewers engaged and eager to see what's next.

3. **The Progress Principle:** Everything in the video should feel as if progress is being made. In other words, it should feel like you're telling the viewer, "Yes, we're getting somewhere with this; stay with me." If a scene or moment doesn't clearly contribute to the feeling of progress, it should be eliminated from the video. Having no lulls or slow spots is key here.

4. **The Payoff Principle:** The whole reason someone watches a video, whether its purpose is to inform or entertain, is to experience a payoff at the end. Similar to a gymnast sticking their landing at the end, you want to do the same with your videos. So much so that just like watching an amazing gymnast, as a viewer, you feel strong emotions—happiness, joy, surprise, disbelief, anger, to name a few—powerful emotions are keys to the Payoff Principal.

5. **The Quit While You're Ahead Principle:** This may sound silly, but it's very important when it comes to short-form video success. Remember, for the algorithm, it's all about retention. This is why, the

second the video's payoff is completed, you should stop the video immediately. Done correctly, you'll find it's not unusual to have videos with a retention rate *over* 100%, meaning your average viewer not only watched the full video, but they watched it a second time as well.

For example, I have a YouTube channel called *Saltwater Fishing University* for offshore fishing. (Yes, I love to fish; you should go with me sometime.) Short-form video has been the catalyst for our success with this channel. What I learned early on is that whenever we create a video showing a fish being caught, as soon as the fish is landed, we need to end the video immediately. If we wait and show the crew celebrating the catch, the retention rates will plummet immediately after the catch.

So even though I enjoyed watching the crew celebrate catching a 700-pound tuna, the rest of the world just wanted to know if the tuna got in the boat. Once it was there, the payoff was done, and the viewers were gone.

As mentioned before, just a few seconds of waste can kill the retention rates for your videos. This is exactly why the Quit While You're Ahead Principle is such a key to success.

Why Does Virality Even Matter?

Finally, you may be thinking to yourself, "But why does virality even matter?"

It's a very legitimate question.

In fact, I used to think virality was a waste of time—just a flashy metric with no real value or impact on the bottom line. But I've learned over the years that virality isn't just about chasing views; it's about the doors it can open, and the signals it creates, for your brand.

Today, there are three major arguments for virality:

1. **Virality creates a massive amount of "signals" for your brand.** Both viewers and AI platforms rely on these "signals" to determine what's worth showing to others. Every like, share, comment, and repeat view sends a signal to the algorithm and users that your content is engaging, valuable, and worth viewing. As we said earlier, the more signals your content generates, the more likely it is to be promoted to a wider audience, and the better it will bode for your brand and business.

2. **Virality drives instant brand awareness.** A *viral video* is easily the fastest and most powerful way in the world to introduce your brand (become known) to a massive number of people in a very short period of time. This kind of exposure isn't just about the numbers; it creates an emotional and memorable connection with your audience. It's why one viral video can literally change the trajectory of a company forever, as people discover and start to associate your brand with value or entertainment.

3. **Virality builds social proof through subscribers.** Viral videos attract a flood of new subscribers, which equates to a significant form of "social proof" online. High subscriber counts signal credibility. The more subscribers you have, the more someone passing by is likely to think, "That many people can't be wrong. I should subscribe to them, too."

16 | Getting Started with Video

I hope that you now share the vision that video isn't just a nice-to-have for your business—it's what today's market demands. More and more, buyers are turning to video to learn, shop, and make decisions. If you're not giving them the dynamic learning experience they crave, they'll keep looking until they find someone who will.

The Selling 7 represents the essential types of videos every business needs to stay competitive and to meet buyers where they are. These videos aren't just about answering questions or showcasing products—they're about building trust, creating connections, and removing barriers to purchase.

Whether you're introducing your team, explaining pricing, or addressing common concerns, these videos will help you stand out in a crowded market and position your business as the best known and most trusted in your space. In this chapter, we'll show you exactly how to get started.

The Selling 7: Planning Videos and Preparing Your Team

The first step to mastering video is getting a clear plan in place. Unlike brainstorming content for The Big 5, identifying The Selling 7 is typically more straightforward. These are the core categories of videos every business needs, tailored to your products, services, and sales process.

Here's how to get started:

1. **Create your video list:** Start by outlining The Selling 7 videos your business needs, prioritizing those that will have the biggest impact. Cost and Price Videos are a natural first step because they address the number-one question buyers ask and are immediately useful for your sales team.

   Next, focus on 80% Videos, which tackle the most common buyer questions and help streamline the sales process. From there, you can move on to Bio Videos, which introduce your team and build trust before the first conversation.

   Complete your list by mapping out the rest of The Selling 7 based on what aligns with your sales and marketing priorities.

2. **Prepare your team for on-camera appearances:** Appearing on camera can feel intimidating, especially for team members who've never done it before. This is where preparation and support make all the difference.

   Start by setting clear expectations. Let your team know their participation is key to creating authentic, effective videos. If they are good with customers, then they can learn to be great on video. It's just a matter of a bit of practice.

   Address any objections or worries, calling back to earlier in the book where we tackled common concerns about being on camera. Reassure your team that buyers trust real people over perfection and that authenticity matters most.

   Finally, equip them with tips and tools to help them feel comfortable and confident on camera. This means taking the time to understand, train, and practice the simple elements (like the "No Stop Rule") that will enable someone to quickly get comfortable on camera. To make this type of training easier for you, we've listed our best on-camera performance tips later in this chapter.

3. **Sort out your equipment and production plan:** You don't need expensive equipment to get started—smartphones, basic lighting, and a tripod can go a long way. That said, investing in a few simple tools, like a high-quality microphone, can significantly improve the quality of your videos.

If there's someone on your team with video experience, lean on their expertise to kickstart production. And if you're considering hiring a videographer, know that most businesses excelling with Endless Customers eventually bring on an in-house videographer to produce consistent, high-quality content. We'll discuss this in greater detail in Chapter 25, "Putting the 5 Components of Endless Customers Into Action."

Reader's Resources: New to video or looking for additional guidance? The EC Companion Guide includes tips on video equipment, lighting, on-camera performance, and production planning to set you up for success.

Training the Team for On-Camera Performance

Of the hundreds of companies we've worked with, we've seen very few people who are truly great on camera from the moment they hit "record." This is why it's essential for you and your team to understand that on-camera performance is a skill that must be developed—just like everything else in life.

This reality means you must commit to training your salespeople and subject matter experts (SMEs) to be more effective on camera. You shouldn't simply throw your team member in front of the camera and say, "Go!" Instead, take the time (it doesn't require much at all) to teach them the skills they need to succeed and encourage them to practice.

To get you started, our team created the SIMPLE On-Camera Performance Checklist:

- **Start with a (three-second) smile:** Before you press "record," smile for three seconds and hold that smile into the video as it starts. Taking this one simple action before you start can have a profound effect on your energy and appearance. It's important to start your smile before the camera is rolling so it looks natural when you begin speaking.

- **Imagine the camera is a real person:** Try tricking your brain into seeing a person instead of the camera. In fact, choose a real person to imagine you're talking to when looking into the camera. This will make a massive difference in your tone and confidence. If you're behind the camera, try asking the subject matter expert, "Who is the exact person you are talking to right now?"

- **Momentum—Follow the "No Stop Rule":** You've likely felt the need to be perfect when you're on camera, stopping every time you made a mistake. The thing is, once you've stopped once, you'll continue to mentally stumble on that same point each time trying to get it perfect. Instead, commit to the "No Stop Rule." Just like on live TV or when talking to a prospect in real life, push forward no matter what mistakes you make. Keep your momentum.

  Bonus: The first take is often the most authentic-sounding one. Get this one out fully and you'll give yourself lots of authentic content to work with.

- **Posture matters:** We communicate at our highest level when we stand. By doing this, we can maximize our ability to use nonverbal cues in our message. Everything from the way we gesticulate with our hands to the way we step closer and further from the camera has an impact on what the audience feels—and thus the connection we make.

- **Leverage the power of story:** Since the beginning of time, storytelling has been woven into our culture. Think about it: when someone asks, "How was your weekend?" you naturally respond with a story. No prep is needed; you just go with it. All of us are storytellers. And if you can tell stories on camera, you'll not only feel more relaxed, but your audience will connect with you faster and on a deeper level than ever before.

- **Engage naturally:** This may be the toughest technique for most to master. Many people struggle on camera or on stage because they are more concerned with impressing their audience than connecting with their audience. This is why it's so essential to teach your team (and yourself) to release the need to look or sound smart and instead focus solely on communicating in the warmest, friendliest, most natural tone possible—just as you would if you were talking to a friend in real life.

These skills won't be mastered in a day. But with time, effort, and repetition, you will be amazed at just how confident and engaging many of your team members will become on camera. In fact, we've seen some clients get to the point where they literally had dozens of trained, confident subject matter experts for video, all because they taught them these tips early and stayed consistent over time.

Using AI to Enhance Video Production and Repurposing

AI offers powerful tools to assist with your video production and extend the reach of your content. As we discussed with The Big 5 (see Chapter 10), AI is great for ideation and script creation, helping you quickly identify topics and develop your message. But when it comes to video, its capabilities go even further.

AI can simplify the editing process, turning raw footage into polished, professional-quality videos. It can also generate captions and subtitles, making your videos more accessible and engaging, particularly on platforms like YouTube and social media.

One of AI's greatest advantages is its ability to help you repurpose your content. For example, you can take a long-form video from The Selling 7 and use AI to create short, compelling clips for platforms like Instagram, TikTok, or YouTube Shorts. AI tools can also extract key points from your videos to generate blog posts, social media captions, or other written content that reinforces your message across multiple channels. (Just be aware of what the repurposing rules are for each platform, because that is something that is evolving daily.)

Finally, AI can optimize your videos for virality and SEO by generating click-worthy titles, descriptions, and thumbnails. This ensures your content gets found by the right audience and performs well on platforms where visibility matters most.

Publish, Repurpose, and Extend Your Reach

Once your Selling 7 videos are ready, it's time to publish—but don't stop there. Video isn't just a one-time effort; it's a dynamic tool that can work for your business across multiple platforms and formats.

Start by publishing your videos where they'll make the biggest impact on the buyer's journey:

- **Your website:** Embed Selling 7 videos on product and service pages, FAQ sections, your video library, and landing pages to enhance the customer experience and answer questions upfront.
- **The sales process:** Incorporate videos into your team's email signatures and follow-up communications to build trust and clarity with prospects.
- **YouTube channel:** Upload your videos to YouTube with SEO-friendly titles and descriptions to extend their reach and position your brand as a trusted authority.

From there, think about how video fits into your larger content strategy. Videos published on your website or YouTube can be shared across social media channels to broaden their reach. Consider turning stand-alone videos into a series that keeps your audience coming back for more, whether it's a weekly Q&A session, product walkthroughs, or customer stories.

The Selling 7 and other videos give your business a way to visually educate buyers and introduce them to your team—all without the need for a formal sales meeting. With video as a foundational tool, you're not just building trust—you're empowering buyers to engage with your brand on their terms.

Next, we'll explore how to take this approach further by refining your sales process and embracing tools and strategies that make for better buying experiences.

Sell How Others Aren't Willing to Sell

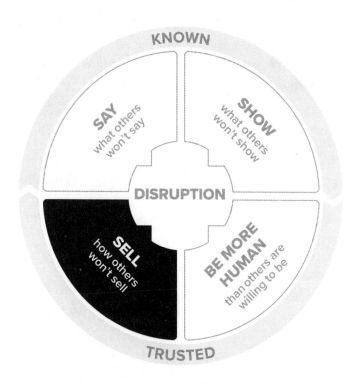

Selling isn't what it used to be.

I remember standing in front of a room full of CEOs from the boating industry in 2018. These weren't just any CEOs—they were leaders of some of the biggest brands in the space, people who had dominated the market for years. During my presentation, I told them something they weren't ready to hear:

"The day is coming when every single one of you is going to have a 'build and price your boat' tool on your website as a manufacturer."

I felt the room freeze.

Some CEOs even laughed.

One went so far as to say, "Well, you're not my buyer anyway."

The irony? I already owned a boat similar to the ones his company sold and was actively shopping for another.

But I knew where the industry was heading. I'd seen firsthand how buyers were growing frustrated, having to jump through hoops just to get basic pricing information. So I stood firm, looked around the room, and said, "One of you will do it. One of you will put that pricing calculator on your site, and when you do, you'll change the rules of the game."

Because here's the truth: **Rule-breakers become rule-makers.**

Sure enough, one of them—Sportsman Boats—took the leap. They became the first major boating manufacturer to offer a build-and-price tool on their site.

The result? They completely disrupted the industry. Buyers flocked to them because they were finally giving customers what everyone else was afraid to provide—transparent pricing information early in the sales process.

Today, it's almost humorous to see many of those same manufacturers who dismissed that prediction now following suit, implementing similar tools on their websites.

They had no choice.

The market demanded it.

The story of Sportsman Boats perfectly illustrates the next pillar of becoming a known and trusted brand: being willing to sell in ways no one else is willing to sell.

The traditional sales process—one where buyers rely heavily on salespeople to guide their journey—is disappearing. **Today, buyers want to be in control.** They crave transparency, autonomy, and tools that let them make decisions on their own terms. Think about how you buy and the experience you want as a consumer—that's exactly what you should be giving your buyers.

And that's why the third pillar of becoming a known and trusted brand is: **Sell in ways others aren't willing to sell.** It's about empowering buyers through education, transparency, and self-service. It's about putting them first, even when it's uncomfortable or unconventional.

In this section, we'll dive into the future of selling. You'll learn how self-service tools can give buyers the control they demand, why involving your sales team in content creation matters, and how AI is reshaping the role of the modern seller.

Along the way, we'll explore real-world examples—like Bahler Brothers and Shasta Pools—that show how these principles drive trust, loyalty, and revenue. And by the end, you'll be equipped with the strategies to build a sales process that aligns with how buyers want to buy—earning their trust and winning their business.

17 | Empower Buyers Through Self-Service

The future of sales is here, and it's all about giving a sense of *control* to the buyer.

A recent study should make any company pause when considering its sales process. **According to Gartner, 75% of buyers would prefer to have a "seller-free" sales experience.**[1]

Yes, 75%.

And just like all these other trends, this number is growing too.

For the record, I don't believe this study means that buyers and consumers dislike salespeople. Rather, it means they don't want to work with a salesperson until they feel they're *ready* to talk to a salesperson.

And when is "ready?" It's when the buyer feels informed and prepared enough to avoid making a buying mistake. Only *then* do most buyers want to talk to a salesperson.

This leaves businesses with a choice. They can complain about this trend, call it "less human," and fight against the rising tide. Or they can live in the solution and use the trend to their advantage, even amplifying the "human" element of selling while providing a more "touchless sale."

How is this possible? Control. And what I mean by control is that you need to give your buyers more control during the buying process. After all, that's what every buyer wants—to feel like they are designing and shaping their own destiny, without the traditional pressures of working with a salesperson.

What is the best way to do this? Through what we refer to as "self-service"—a megatrend that will affect sales and marketing in dramatic ways for years to come.

What Is a Self-Service Tool?

Self-service enables buyers to independently navigate key aspects of the purchasing process—from information gathering to making decisions—*without being forced to speak to a human.*

In other words, when you implement self-service correctly, you take what was previously a human interaction with sales or customer service and allow buyers to achieve the same results by simply engaging with your website. (Don't worry, we'll discuss how you still retain the human aspect of your business in the next section.)

Think about how *you* shop. For instance, when you're in the market for real estate or a new car, how often do you prefer to do your own research before talking to a salesperson? If you're like most people, you want to handle it on your own terms, at your own pace, and only engage with someone when you're ready.

Your customers are no different. They want the same freedom to explore and decide on their own timeline. Implementing self-service tools not only empowers them, but these tools also help move the prospective buyer closer to a purchase.

And if that kind of experience takes place on your website, who are they likely to buy from?

Yes, you.

Embracing a more seller-free approach with self-service tools brings three undeniable benefits:

1. **Self-service has a dramatic impact on lead generation, often becoming the fastest path to doubling lead flow.** I'm not exaggerating here. Consistently, companies tell us how amazed they are at how quickly their first self-service tool starts generating a significant increase in leads.

2. **Self-service gives your company a serious competitive edge.** Buyers crave it, and most businesses aren't willing to provide it

(because, once again, it means you'll have to be willing to do what the rest of your industry is not willing to do).

3. **Engaging in a self-service tool increases the sunk costs on the part of the consumer.** This means the more invested they are in "designing" their buyer's journey with your tools, the more likely they are to buy from you.

If you're confused right now about any of these benefits, it will become more clear as you read the rest of this chapter and learn about the **5 Types of Self-Service Tools** that will have a massive impact on sales and marketing in the years ahead.

Give Buyers Control: The 5 Types of Self-Service Tools

Let's take a look at what "seller-free" looks like in practice. There are five main self-service tools you should be considering:

1. **Self-Assessment:** These tools, like quizzes or scorecards, allow buyers to assess their needs and challenges. They provide personalized insights and recommendations, empowering prospects with clear next steps before ever speaking to your sales team.

2. **Self-Selection:** To help overwhelmed buyers find exactly what they need, these interactive tools ask targeted questions to guide prospects to their ideal solution, building trust through personalized recommendations rather than overwhelming them with options.

3. **Self-Configurator:** Buyers want to visualize how a product or service will fit into their world. These tools allow them to personally build or create the thing they're looking to buy, turning abstract possibilities into concrete plans while deepening their investment in the outcome.

4. **Self-Scheduling:** By removing the back-and-forth of scheduling, these tools give buyers control over setting appointments or demos. They streamline the process, create a frictionless experience, and can even allow prospects to choose the team member they want to meet.

5. **Self-Pricing:** Pricing calculators and estimators—the most important elements on the list—give buyers the transparency they crave. By providing ranges or estimates, these tools set clear budget expectations and reduce friction, establishing trust and moving buyers closer to a purchase decision.

5 Types of Self-Service Tools

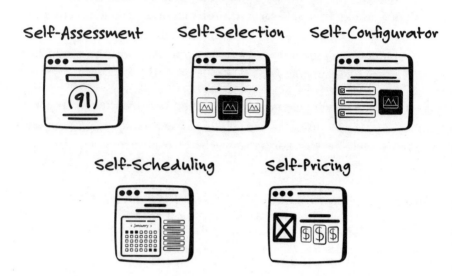

Self-Assessment   Self-Selection   Self-Configurator

Self-Scheduling   Self-Pricing

Each of these tools represents a shift in how buyers want to interact with businesses today—on their terms, with clarity and control. They're not just conveniences; they're trust builders, momentum drivers, and ultimately sales accelerators.

Let's dive into the first one: self-assessment tools, which empower buyers to understand where they stand and what they need—before they ever reach out to you.

Tool 1: Self-Assessment Tools

"Where do I stand?"

Self-assessment tools, like quizzes or questionnaires, are simple yet powerful ways to help prospects understand their current position, identify gaps, and realize the potential benefits of making a change.

On a personal level, one of the most life-changing self-assessment tools I encountered was Website Grader, created by HubSpot founder Dharmesh Shah in 2009. It allowed anyone to get a "score" for their website, measuring its alignment with Inbound Marketing best practices.

That same year, we were fighting to save our swimming pool company. I stumbled upon Website Grader and was immediately curious to see how our site, www.RiverPoolsandSpas.com, would score. When I took the test, we received a 17 out of 100. It was a wake-up call. I thought, "There's no way I'm going to accept having a website this bad! 17? You have got to be kidding me!"

Determined to improve, we followed the tool's recommendations. Over the next few months, we kept adding content and features to our website. And each day, I'd return to Website Grader to check our progress. (Yes, I was a little obsessed!)

The best part of this experience was the sense of control it gave me. I didn't need an advisor to point out my site's shortcomings. The tool provided a clear score, actionable steps, and the freedom to improve at my own pace.

Isn't that what every buyer wants? Isn't that what you want? This is exactly why self-assessment tools are so powerful.

Website Grader became a major catalyst for HubSpot's early growth. Dharmesh Shah's goal was to empower potential customers without forcing them to buy or learn in traditional ways—and it worked.

The same principle applies to you and your prospects. When you provide a self-assessment tool that gives a score, rating, or grade—along with personalized recommendations and actionable steps—it empowers users to make meaningful improvements.

To illustrate this, here are examples of different types of self-assessment tools:

- **Financial health check:** A financial advisory firm could create an interactive tool that asks prospects about their income, expenses, savings, and investments. The tool would then provide a "financial health score," highlighting areas for potential improvement, such as emergency fund sufficiency or retirement planning.

- **Home energy audit tool:** A company in the home improvement or sustainable energy space could develop a self-assessment tool that evaluates a homeowner's energy consumption and efficiency. By answering questions about insulation, appliances, and energy habits, users would receive a report on their energy efficiency and specific actions they can take to save money and reduce energy use.

- **Employee engagement survey:** A consulting firm specializing in organizational development could offer a self-assessment tool that HR departments can use to measure the current level of employee engagement. The tool would ask questions about workplace culture, leadership communication, and job satisfaction, providing a score and tips for boosting engagement.

- **Cybersecurity risk assessment:** An IT security company could create a tool that asks businesses about their current cybersecurity measures, such as password policies, employee training, and network protections. The tool would generate a risk score and recommendations for enhancing their cybersecurity posture.
- **Sales process evaluation:** A sales training and coaching company could offer a self-assessment tool for sales teams to gauge the effectiveness of their current processes. It could include questions on lead nurturing, closing strategies, and follow-up practices, providing a score and customized tips to improve their sales cycle.

Are you seeing the possibilities? There are certainly many. When these tools are done correctly, prospects will often refer back to their "score" when talking with your sales team. Furthermore, your sales team is able to see their "score" before the first sales meeting, again making the usage of such a tool a massive win-win.

Tool 2: Self-Selection Tools

▌ "What is the best option for me?"

We've all experienced that moment—faced with too many choices and unsure of which to pick. Whether it's selecting a software platform, choosing a health insurance plan, or picking a fitness tracker, it's easy to feel overwhelmed by the sheer number of options. But as buyers, we don't just want any solution; we want the one that fits our specific needs. And most savvy consumers know that just because one option worked for someone else, it doesn't mean it's the best choice for them.

That's where self-selection tools come into play.

A self-selection tool guides prospects through the decision-making process when there's a choice to be made, narrowing down their options so they can confidently choose the solution that fits them best. It removes guesswork and empowers buyers to make informed decisions, while also speeding up the sales process for your team.

At River Pools, for example, we offer a tool that helps potential pool buyers answer the question "What is the best type of inground pool for me?" With three main types to choose from—fiberglass, concrete, or vinyl liner—this tool simplifies the decision by asking questions tailored to the buyer's needs, lifestyle, and preferences.

What makes this tool so powerful is its honesty. Every day, it tells dozens of potential customers that our product (fiberglass pools) might not be the best fit for them based on their unique needs.

Can you imagine recommending on your own website that someone should *not* buy your product and instead should go with a competitor's? This is the essence of saying, showing, and selling in a way that no one else in your industry dares to do.

But as radical as it sounds, this level of transparency drives immense trust. The key to all of this, though, is that you have to design the tool in a way that is honest and unbiased.

Start with a question with which your sales team is often confronted that involves a choice. In fact, you can use the phrase "What is the best _____ for me?" as a prompt. Once you've chosen the question, simply ask yourself, "If one of our salespeople was asked this by a prospect, what questions would we ask to give them an answer or recommendation?"

To get your ideas flowing, here are some examples of potential self-selection tools in a variety of industries:

Home Renovation and Improvement

- **Flooring selector tool:** This tool helps homeowners choose the best type of flooring based on their lifestyle, budget, and preferences (e.g., durability, ease of cleaning, design aesthetics).
- **Paint color picker:** This interactive tool lets users input room type, lighting, and desired ambiance to get tailored paint color recommendations.

Healthcare Services

- **Health insurance plan selector:** This tool guides users through selecting the best health insurance plan based on their medical needs, budget, and family size.

- **Symptom checker tool:** Provided by clinics or telehealth platforms, this tool asks users about their symptoms and suggests potential care options (e.g., virtual visit, in-person appointment, over-the-counter treatment).

Technology and Software

- **SaaS (software as a service) product chooser:** This tool helps businesses or individuals determine the best software plan or package based on the features they need, the number of users, and the type of work they do.
- **Device compatibility checker:** Tech retailers can use this tool to allow consumers to input the specs of their current device to check if new software or hardware is compatible.

Retail and Ecommerce

- **Clothing fit finder:** This online tool for fashion retailers helps shoppers determine their ideal size based on measurements, body shape, and style preferences.
- **Gift selector tool:** With this ecommerce tool, users can find the perfect gift based on the recipient's interests, age, and occasion.

By offering an unbiased self-selection tool, you're not just helping your prospects make a confident choice—you're demonstrating that you're the most trustworthy source in your market.

Even better, when used properly, your sales team will often hear, "I used that tool on your website and I already know what I want"—something that is certainly music to a salesperson's ears.

And that's what the Endless Customers journey is all about.

Tool 3: Self-Configurator Tools

"What Will It Look Like?"

When you have the opportunity to design, build, or customize something before making a purchase, what's the impact? It goes beyond just selecting features—it's about experiencing a deeper sense of control and a personal connection to the product. When you're the one holding the paintbrush, your emotional investment in the final outcome skyrockets.

That's the magic of a self-configurator tool.

Self-configurator tools let buyers move from abstract ideas to concrete visions by designing and personalizing a product to fit their needs. This process doesn't just help them visualize the outcome; it makes them more committed to it. They're no longer buying *a product*—they're buying *their product*.

Think about cars. Would you rather buy *a car*, or would you rather buy *your car*? See the difference?

We all have a natural desire to create, to build something that's uniquely ours—whether it's for our personal lives or our business. And the more control we feel over that creation, the more invested we become.

Here are some examples of what self-configurator tools might look like in different industries:

Home Improvement

- **Custom cabinet configurator:** This tool helps homeowners design kitchen or bathroom cabinetry by choosing dimensions, materials, finishes, and additional features like soft-close drawers or pull-out shelves.

Landscaping

- **Landscape design tool:** With this configurator, landscaping companies can allow clients to design their outdoor space by selecting plants, paving materials, water features, and garden layouts.

Financial Services

- **Insurance policy configurator:** This tool guides users in building a custom insurance policy by selecting coverage options, deductibles, and additional riders.

Education and E-learning

- **Curriculum planner:** This tool for educational institutions or training providers lets learners customize their course schedule by choosing subjects, modules, and elective options.

These examples are just the beginning of a future that's full of incredible self-service technology. As augmented and virtual reality continues to become more accessible, brands will have even more opportunities to integrate self-configurators into their marketing. Imagine prospects being able to see *their* customized product in real-time, in their space, before making a purchase—an experience your competitors simply can't match.

You've heard the famous phrase "If you build it, they will come." In the case of self-configurator tools, it's more like "Let them build it, and they will come."

Tool 4: Self-Scheduling Tools

"When can we meet?"

The fastest company often wins the sale. The saying "time kills all deals" has never been more relevant than in today's market.

If there's one thing that can derail a deal in the modern buyer's journey, it's the back-and-forth over email or phone trying to schedule a sales appointment. Scheduling should be fast and seamless for your prospects, but too often it's not.

We've all been there: We're excited to talk to a company about a product or service, only to find ourselves caught in an endless loop of calls or emails just to set up a meeting. The hassle becomes frustrating, and real engagement never happens.

This is where self-scheduling tools come into play. These tools allow prospects to book appointments directly based on availability and preferences, cutting out the traditional back-and-forth and removing the need for human interaction. Here are some potential examples of self-scheduling tools:

Healthcare

- **Doctor appointment scheduler:** Patients can book appointments with doctors, specialists, or therapists based on their availability, preferred location, and urgency of the visit.

Professional Services

- **Financial advisor meeting scheduler:** Clients can book meetings with financial advisors based on their availability and choose between in-person or virtual sessions.
- **Law firm consultation scheduler:** Clients of legal practices can schedule initial consultations with specific lawyers, select meeting types, and provide basic case details in advance.

Corporate and B2B Services

- **Sales demo scheduler:** Potential clients can schedule product demos or discovery calls with a sales team, allowing them to choose representatives and times that suit them best.
- **Client onboarding scheduler:** Businesses can schedule onboarding sessions with new clients, ensuring that both parties can choose times that align with their availability.

Self-scheduling tools give potential customers a sense of "I'm in control," and as we've discussed before, this is exactly what every buyer wants.

You can even take it a step further by letting prospects not only schedule time with your sales team but also choose which salesperson they want to work with.

We've conducted multiple tests with various clients, and the results have been stunning. Allowing someone to pick their own salesperson (from a list that includes names, photos, bios, and personal videos) has consistently *doubled* the close rates.

Yes, you read that right—allowing prospects to choose *who* they work with doubles your company's overall close rate. Once again, it's all about giving the customer a sense of control. Control means trust, and trust means more sales.

Tool 5: Self-Pricing Tools

"How much does it cost?"

Self-pricing tools, often called pricing calculators or pricing estimators, are built to answer the fundamental question every buyer has. But it's not just about "How much does it cost?"—it's about answering questions like:

- "Can we even afford this?"
- "What price range are we looking at here?"
- "What factors drive the costs of this product or service?"

After working on hundreds of pricing calculator implementations across countless industries, we can confidently say that pricing tools are one of the fastest ways to build trust and generate more leads for your sales team, for two reasons:

1. **Every buyer—B2B or B2C—wants at least a price range** to assess affordability and decide if they should engage further.
2. **Most companies still avoid talking about pricing on their websites,** leaving buyers in the dark when transparency is what they crave. By offering a pricing estimator, you're stepping up and doing what others won't: saying, showing, and selling with transparency.

At IMPACT, we recently worked with a home improvement company facing lagging sales. With their peak season approaching—a critical 90-day window when they typically gain 75% of their annual leads—they needed a fast turnaround. We knew no contractor in their market had a pricing tool on their site, so we quickly developed one.

The results? Year-over-year, their leads in May jumped from 200 to 700—a 350% increase, despite a market downturn. This tool became a game-changer, fueling their buyer journey and overall success. It cost less than $25,000 to build and generated over $1 million in additional revenue.

That's serious ROI.

This example also highlights how quickly you can see results from implementing the Endless Customers System. While building momentum with online content can take time, self-service tools—especially pricing estimators—often deliver immediate results.

Key Tips for Effective Pricing Estimators

A common mistake with pricing estimators is failing to educate prospects about their choices. If buyers are presented with options—such as different patio stones—without clear photos and explanations, confusion follows. Don't assume prospects know more than they do. Include "learn more" links, videos, or articles to guide them, just as you would in a live sales conversation.

Also, you don't need to provide an exact price. A price range is often sufficient to answer, "Can I afford this?" or "Is this within budget?" Boost your calculator's value by showing not just upfront costs but long-term expenses, especially if your product's appeal grows over time. Adding features like "monthly payment" or financing options can further enhance engagement and build confidence.

Building Your First Pricing Tool

When companies get excited about implementing pricing estimators, the next question is often, "Where do we start?"

You have two main options:

1. **A customized solution** tailored for your business
2. **An out-of-the-box solution** that you can quickly integrate into your site

Both have their merits, but if your budget allows, a custom-built tool is the better route. This is a service we offer at IMPACT, with numerous case studies to prove its success.

If you need something quick and budget-friendly with less customization, I've developed an AI-powered pricing calculator that has now been used by companies all over the world and can be added to your website in under 30 minutes. Most users see an immediate boost in qualified leads and are shocked at just how quickly they see results. Visit www.priceguide.ai to learn more.

Pulling Back the Curtain: Great Examples of Self-Service Tools

Although we as buyers love them and self-selection tools have proven to be highly effective, too few companies are taking full advantage of them. The ones that do are the ones truly living The 4 Pillars of a Known and Trusted Brand, and they're setting themselves apart from the competition.

Here are a few standout examples that truly bring self-service tools to life. You'll notice some of these companies focused on a single self-service tool and executed it exceptionally well while others combined multiple tools to deliver an even more comprehensive experience.

Bahler Brothers' Self-Assessment Tool

Bahler Brothers is a landscaping company based in Connecticut. Their patio design style quiz is accessible directly from their navigation bar, and everything is conveniently located on a single page of their website.

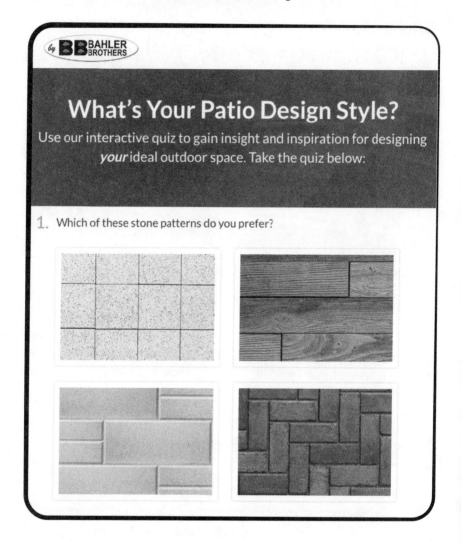

Bahler Brothers truly wants to understand how you're going to use the space. To accomplish this, they offer a series of questions that help you determine the style of patio you should build based on your preferences.

They don't stop at simply asking the question, though. What Bahler Brothers did well is that for each question, they showed different images of products and spaces they have produced and asked, "Which of these styles and spaces resonates with you?" This visual approach is incredibly engaging for potential customers.

6. Which of these spaces would you like to spend time with friends and family?

7. If you could add one of these features to your yard, which would it be?

One particularly impressive aspect is their ability to blend visual inspiration with practical questions, making the tool both user-friendly and insightful.

And to make sure they're able to convert visitors into leads, they end their quiz with a form, collecting your name and email. After you fill it out, they immediately share your patio design style with you.

At this point, there's no pressure to buy. You can view their design services or continue to explore and educate yourself. It's really well done and serves as an excellent example of an effective self-assessment tool. I highly recommend checking it out.

AIS Self-Selection and Self-Pricing Tool

Another tool I often share as an example is the one we helped our friends at AIS build for their buyers. AIS provides office technology solutions for businesses of all kinds, both large and small. Their self-selection tool is a prime example of how to guide customers in choosing the right copier or printer.

Manufacturers in the industry had previously created tools similar to this but had done a poor job; they were extremely self-serving. AIS was the first in their industry to create a tool that encompassed products from several manufacturers. Without bias, they can truly point users in the right direction without requiring them to speak to a salesperson first—a tremendous benefit for today's independent buyers.

The tool starts by clearly stating its purpose: helping you find a printer or copier that meets all of *your* needs. It then takes you through a series of questions, showing your progress with each step, which keeps you engaged and informed along the way.

AIS understands that different customers have different needs. They ask targeted questions about the functions you require—whether you need to print, copy, or both. They also inquire about your paper usage, such as how many sheets of paper you plan to use per month.

But AIS doesn't stop at just asking questions. The tool includes visual elements, allowing users to choose between black-and-white or color options, which makes the decision-making process even more intuitive.

At the end of the questionnaire, the tool suggests specific products that meet the user's criteria. What's more, it includes price ranges for the recommended solutions, so users can immediately understand the potential investment they're looking at. This transparency helps buyers feel more confident and prepared before moving forward.

If you decide to make a purchase, the tool seamlessly directs you to their ecommerce store, once again without requiring a conversation with a salesperson.

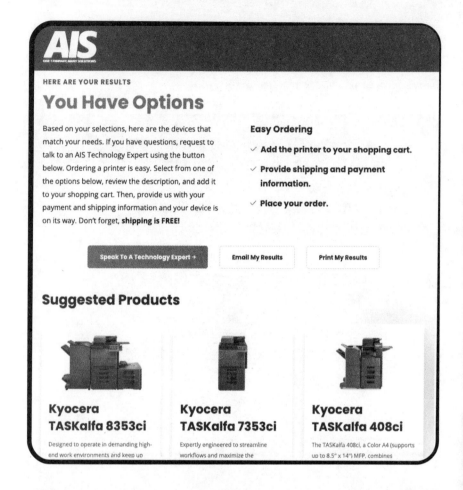

AIS did an outstanding job. It's a well-executed example of an effective self-selection tool that prioritizes the buyer's needs and delivers an engaging experience.

Shasta Pools: Self-Configurator and Self-Pricing Tool

When it comes to buying a pool, the process can be overwhelming. Prospective buyers are often faced with a multitude of options, features, and upgrades—all without a clear understanding of what these choices entail or how much they might cost.

Recognizing this pain point, Shasta Pools, a Phoenix-based pool builder, decided to break from tradition and address these concerns head-on. The traditional approach to pricing—providing a vague quote after a long consultation—wasn't working for today's informed buyers. The challenge was clear: How do you empower customers to explore their options without overwhelming them?

To do this, Shasta Pools collaborated with IMPACT to create a tool that acts as both a pricing calculator and a configurator, educating customers every step of the way and allowing them to design their ideal pool while understanding the costs associated with each choice.

Here's how it works. Customers simply visit the Shasta Pools website and navigate to the pool estimator page. There, they are guided through a simple, nine-step process where they can configure their pool by answering a series of questions. These questions cover everything from pool shape, entry and interior finishes, water features, and decking, allowing customers to build their perfect pool design.

The tool provides detailed explanations, images, and videos for each option, helping users understand what every choice entails. This approach mimics a real sales appointment, giving customers the knowledge they need to choose confidently.

The results of this dual-function tool on Shasta Pools' business speak for themselves. Shortly after launching the tool, more than 50% of all first appointments being scheduled involved customers who used the pricing calculator.

In one month alone, Shasta Pools scheduled 166 families to meet with a sales designer, and 83 of them had already priced out their pool using the calculator. This level of prequalification is leading to more efficient and effective meetings, because customers are coming in educated and prepared.

For context, the average price of a pool in Arizona ranges between $55,000 and $80,000—a significant investment for most families. By offering this tool, Shasta Pools is not only streamlining the sales process but also creating peace of mind for customers making a big, permanent investment.

Final Thoughts on Self-Service Tools

In the coming years, self-service tools won't be a competitive advantage—they'll be a necessity. Every serious business will need tools like pricing estimators, self-assessment quizzes, and configurators on their websites. Why? Because technology will make it easier to implement, and buyers will demand it.

Please do not wait for the market to push you into action.

The businesses that will thrive will be the ones that act now—those willing to sell in ways that others in their industry aren't. By giving buyers the tools they need to feel informed, in control, and empowered, you position your business as the most trusted voice in your space.

Remember, no buyer ever says, "I just wish I could talk to more salespeople."

What they *do* want is a seamless, frictionless experience that allows them to make decisions at their own pace. When you provide that, you're not just meeting their expectations—you're exceeding them.

Self-service tools don't replace the human element of selling; they enhance it.

By removing the repetitive, time-consuming steps from the buyer's journey, these tools free up your sales team to focus on what they do best: building relationships and closing deals. Meanwhile, your buyers are more confident, informed, and ready to make a decision—leading to faster sales cycles, higher close rates, and greater customer satisfaction.

The time to start with self-service tools is now.

Evaluate your current sales process. What questions or challenges do your buyers face repeatedly? Which interactions could be streamlined with a self-service tool? Begin with just one—whether it's a pricing calculator, a self-scheduling tool, or a configurator—and commit to doing it well.

Reader's Resources: Looking to create self-service tools that captivate your buyers and streamline their journey? Check out the EC Companion Guide to find the latest examples of successful tools, actionable tips for building your own, and insights into design, implementation, and functionality.

18

Sell Faster and Better with Assignment Selling

Back when I was selling pools, I stumbled upon something that completely transformed the way we approached sales. It all started with a simple question: *What was the difference between prospects who bought pools from us and those who didn't?*

Curious, I dove into our HubSpot analytics to compare the behavior of two groups—buyers and non-buyers. Both had requested quotes through our website, but their paths diverged dramatically from there.

The data revealed a stunning insight: If a prospect consumed 30 or more pages of our website before their first sales appointment, they bought 80% of the time. But those who didn't hit that 30-page threshold? Our close rate plummeted to just 25%—the industry average.

That was my lightbulb moment.

The data couldn't have been clearer: Prospects who consumed 30 pieces of our content were four times more likely to buy.

Four times! That's when I realized the power of educating buyers early.

We wasted no time. We immediately revamped our sales process at River Pools. No more rushing to give quotes through quick qualifying calls.

Instead, we made content the centerpiece of our strategy. From that point forward, every prospect had to hit that 30-page threshold before we'd schedule a sales appointment.

The results were game-changing. In just one year, we went from selling 75 pools in 250 appointments (a 30% close rate) to selling 95 pools in just 120 appointments—a staggering 79% close rate.

Our sales team's lives transformed. Gone were the 60-hour weeks and late nights getting home at 11 p.m. Instead, they had balance, focus, and time with their families. And our sales process became more efficient, effective, and enjoyable. All because we used content as a sales accelerator.

I called this approach **Assignment Selling,** and it has helped thousands of companies worldwide transform their sales results.

In this chapter, we'll explore what makes Assignment Selling so effective, how to build a sales process that supports it, the step-by-step method for implementation, and how to embed it into your company culture.

Assignment Selling

Assignment Selling is the strategic practice of requiring prospects to consume specific educational content before sales conversations to improve close rates and reduce sales cycles.

If you talk with anyone who has been selling for a long time and ask them, "Are there certain questions that, when you receive them from a prospect, you can immediately tell they're not informed enough to buy?"

Most salespeople will immediately reply "Absolutely" to this.

For example, when I was a pool guy, if someone asked me in the home, "Marcus, what's the difference between a fiberglass and a concrete swimming pool?" I knew I was in trouble, because this person hadn't invested enough time to become educated enough to make a buying decision.

In other words, **a lack of education equals not ready to buy.**

This is why Assignment Selling is so valuable. When done properly, it means a salesperson will spend less time "teaching" (answering basic questions the prospect should already know) and more time "selling"—something every salesperson would prefer.

The way this is accomplished is by assigning specific content—whether it's articles, videos, or self-service tools—to consume before a sales conversation, so the prospect is more informed and ready to buy.

Assignment Selling allows you to spend less time educating and more time selling.

Having taught Assignment Selling to so many companies across various industries, we've never seen a situation where it didn't improve closing rates. Just like it worked for River Pools, it will work for you.

In order for Assignment Selling to truly work, though, you'll need to assign the right content at the right stage of the sales process. For some organizations, this is problematic, simply because they don't have a clearly defined sales process.

So before we discuss the details of doing Assignment Selling the right way, let's briefly make sure your sales process is rock-solid.

Why Your Sales Process Matters

Sales today are rarely a "one-call close." Instead, buyers generally move through a series of decisions and touchpoints, each one bringing them closer to a "yes."

A typical sales process looks something like this:

- Lead generation/prospecting
- Initial contact
- Qualification
- Needs analysis
- Presentation/demonstration
- Handling objections
- Proposal/quotation
- Negotiation
- Closing
- Follow-up/post-sale

The issue? Roughly 50% of organizations don't have a defined sales process. This makes Assignment Selling very difficult. Why? Because buyers move through different phases, with each phase requiring a different "need" or "type" of information to address where the buyer is in that moment.

For Assignment Selling to be effective, you need to deliver the right content at the right time. Without a clear sales process, companies end up assigning content that doesn't truly match the buyer's stage, yielding minimal impact.

Defining Your Sales Process

I'm not here to write another book on creating a sales process. Instead, I'll share a few key principles and actionable steps to help you refine your process and set yourself up for Assignment Selling success.

Before diving into the specifics of how to build your sales process, let's be clear about what a "defined sales process" is:

> *A defined sales process is a clearly documented, systematic, and repeatable approach that guides sales teams through each stage of converting a prospect into a customer. It maps out the specific actions, milestones, and requirements that must be met at each stage, ensuring consistency in how deals progress and how the sales team engages with prospects.*

You may already have a defined sales process—or many of you may not. Either way, know this: **A strong process is essential if you want your team to start "selling in ways others aren't willing to sell."**

Without a process, you've got the Wild West. That doesn't mean you should stifle sales creativity. It does mean you need a framework that provides clear steps, defined stages, structured actions, and consistent language to guide your team toward success.

With that in mind, let's dive into the four steps to creating an effective sales process.

Four Steps to Creating an Effective Sales Process

Crafting a process that aligns with your buyers' journey and empowers your team to engage with consistency and purpose is the key to driving better results.

By following these four steps, you'll create a sales process that not only works but also sets the stage for integrating Assignment Selling seamlessly.

Step 1: Map Your Buyer's Journey

Every sale follows a predictable path, often referred to as the buyer's journey. This journey is the roadmap your prospects take as they move from recognizing a problem to making a purchase decision.

To build an effective sales process, you need to understand what drives your buyers at each stage:

- **Awareness:** What questions are they asking as they first begin researching their problem? What pain points are motivating them to explore solutions?
- **Consideration:** How are they comparing their options? What criteria are they using to evaluate you versus your competitors?
- **Decision:** What specific factors influence their final choice? What objections might arise, and how can you address them?

The better you understand these stages, the more effectively you can align your sales process to match the needs of your prospects.

Step 2: Define Your Sales Stages

Outline clear stages that guide your team through each milestone in the sales process. While the number of stages can vary—anywhere from three to 12—the ideal structure typically includes around eight steps.

For example, a typical sales process might include:

1. Secure appointment
2. Identify need
3. Present solution
4. Post-presentation
5. Closed won/lost

Reader's Resources: Use the buyer's journey map in the EC Companion Guide to document key questions and decision drivers at each stage. Scan the QR code to download a copy of the template.

Each stage should have clear entry and exit criteria to ensure smooth progression. For example, an entry criterion for the "identify need" stage might be that the prospect has requested an initial consultation, while the exit criterion could be when the sales rep has gathered enough information to tailor a solution or proposal.

Key point: Avoid rigidly tying stages to required calls or meetings. Some buyers are ready to move quickly while others need more time. Your sales process should adapt to meet buyers where they are, creating a seamless experience for them and greater efficiency for your team.

Reader's Resources: For a sample sales process with entry and exit criteria, check out the EC Companion Guide. This resource offers a practical template you can use or customize to suit your business.

Step 3: Document Your Process

Think of your sales process like a pilot's checklist—focus on the essential actions that keep the plane moving forward. Don't overcomplicate it; simplicity is key.

- List the key activities for each stage of your process.
- Define clear success criteria so your team knows exactly what success looks like at each milestone.
- Regularly update the process based on results, learning from what works and refining what doesn't.

By documenting and refining your process, you'll ensure everyone on your team is aligned and working toward the same goals.

Step 4: Train Your Team and Implement

Your sales process is only as effective as your team's ability to consistently execute it. To ensure success:

- Provide thorough training, so your team fully understands the process and can confidently apply it.
- Practice through role-play, giving them the opportunity to refine their approach and build confidence.
- Offer regular feedback to maintain consistency and keep everyone aligned with the process.
- Continuously update the process (and retrain your team) based on real-world experiences, ensuring it stays relevant and effective.

Once your team is trained and aligned, it's time to implement. A solid process is your foundation, but consistency in execution is what truly drives results.

Now, let's explore how Assignment Selling fits into each stage of your process. Think of your sales process as the roadmap, and Assignment Selling as the vehicle that moves prospects forward more effectively.

How to Implement Assignment Selling in Your Sales Process

Your content strategy should align with your prospect's buying journey, delivering the right information at the right time (ideally being all the content and tools you've read about up to this point in the book).

And remember: A prospect's willingness to consume content directly correlates with their readiness to buy. Start small—even a one-minute video can significantly boost engagement.

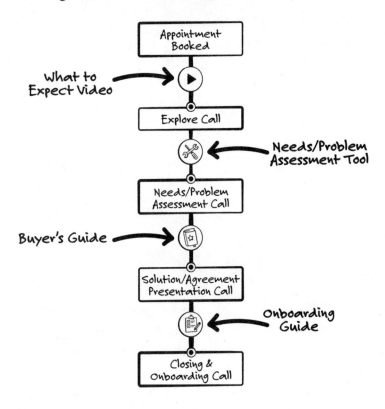

Assignment Selling Content Map

- Appointment Booked
- What to Expect Video →
- Explore Call
- Needs/Problem Assessment Tool →
- Needs/Problem Assessment Call
- Buyer's Guide →
- Solution/Agreement Presentation Call
- Onboarding Guide →
- Closing & Onboarding Call

Keep in mind that the following list is not all-inclusive, but you can at least use it as a guide to get started.

Content before first appointment: Speed and personalization are critical here. Studies show that responding within five minutes makes you 100 times more likely to connect versus waiting 30 minutes. Provide your prospective buyer with the following:

- **Bio Video:** Quick personal introduction.
- **What to Expect Video:** Clear overview of the first meeting. Your goal is to become the appointment they're most excited about.

Content to assess and define needs: Help prospects gain clarity through:

- **Interactive Self-Assessments:** Guide them to self-identify gaps or needs.
- **Cost/Price Content:** Quantify the cost of inaction versus change. When you're the most helpful resource, prospects naturally gravitate to you over competitors.

Content to understand options: As prospects evaluate choices, you should provide:

- **Buyer's Guide:** Compare features and benefits.
- **Pricing Education:** Explain industry value drivers.
- **Product/Service-Fit Video:** Show your solution in action. This stage builds consistency—ensure every team member delivers the same message through approved content.

Content before presentation: Here is where you can reinforce confidence with:

- **80% Video:** Address common questions.
- **Claims We Make Video:** Validate key statements.
- **Customer Journey Video:** Show relatable success stories. But don't overdo it—if they're ready to buy, move forward. Time kills deals.

Content post-sale: Continue building trust through:

- **Welcome Video:** Avoid the chance for immediate buyer's remorse by continuing the excitement after they've purchased.
- **Implementation Guide:** What happens next? How do they prepare for your service or onboard to a product?
- **Regular Updates:** Use email, video, or personal touchpoints to transform a sale into a lasting relationship.

You now know what content to share at each stage of your sales process. But having great content isn't enough—how you assign it makes all the difference. This is where most salespeople fall short. They casually mention content to prospects or weakly suggest "taking a look" at some materials. Instead, you need a proven script that turns content into commitment.

The Assignment Selling Script

The key to effective Assignment Selling lies in perfecting three aspects:

1. **Why it matters:** What is the risk of being uneducated or ignorant about a particular product or service?
2. **What the assignment is:** Be explicit about the task. Leave no room for confusion.
3. **When it's due:** Set a clear deadline to create urgency and ensure timely follow-up.

This is what I call **The 3 Ws of Assignment Selling.**

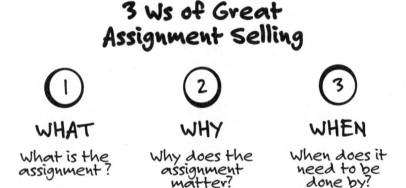

Next, we're going to walk through exactly how to apply The 3 Ws when implementing Assignment Selling. As we go through this, pay close attention to the specifics of the script.

Setting the Stage

Before starting Assignment Selling, a typical call at River Pools would go something like this: "Hey Marcus, I'm checking out your website. Could you come out to my house this Friday and give me a quote for a swimming pool?" And his response was usually, "Yeah, sure, I'll come out."

But once we understood the power of those 30 pages to increase closing rates, that changed. When asked the same question, the response became:

> *"Of course, I'd love to come out and give you a quote. But you're getting ready to spend a lot of money, and if you're going to spend a lot of money, I know you don't want to make any mistakes. So as to ensure you don't make any mistakes, you need to be well-informed and educated. To make this happen, I'm going to send you a couple of things that you're going to love."*

Notice the emphasis on acknowledging that the prospect is about to make a significant financial decision, and we don't want them to make any mistakes. This is your first W of The 3 Ws—*Why*.

It's not about stating the obvious; it's about prompting the prospect to think, "Yeah, I don't want to make any mistakes because I don't know what I should know." It creates a curiosity gap, and the prospect will naturally want to fill that gap. The way that's done, of course, is by completing the assignment.

This line also builds trust because the prospect can see we understood the gravity of their decision. This wasn't just about selling a pool; it was about making sure they felt confident and informed every step of the way.

Just by doing this one thing, you're already selling in a way your competitors likely aren't.

Making the Ask

Now that you've set the stage, it's time to assign the homework. This is where you need to be clear, specific, and direct, driving home all of The 3 Ws. The goal here is to make the assignment feel like a natural and valuable part of the process—not just a hoop to jump through.

Here's what assigning the content sounds like:

> *"To help you get a clear picture of what this process will look like, I'm going to send you an email with two key pieces of content.*
> *"The first is a video that shows you the entire process of a fiberglass swimming pool being installed. You're going to see what it looks like when it arrives at your home, the excavation of the hole, the pool going in the ground, the patio going in around it, and the cleanup. This way, when I come out to your house on Friday, you're not going to ask, 'Marcus, so what does this process look like?' because you're already going to know.*

> *"The second is a guide that covers the most common questions and decisions you'll face, like: Should I get a heater with my pool? What's the best type of heater? Should it be gas? Should it be electric? Should it heat and cool my water? Should I get a cover? What's the best type of cover? And so on."*

At this point, you've explained the "what" and the "why" in very clear and appealing detail.

Now it's time to define "when" and ask for a commitment:

> *"Based on this, Mr. /Mrs. Jones, will you take the time to review these two things before our appointment on Friday?"*

Having had this exact conversation with hundreds of buyers, I can tell you that 90% of the time, the simple response is "Sure."

Ask yourself: How much time would you save in your sales appointments if the most repeated questions you already get asked were eliminated because the prospect had already learned the answers from you?

Twenty minutes? Thirty minutes? Maybe even more?

Now, think about what that would add up to over a year. This is why Assignment Selling is extraordinary when it comes to adding efficiency to any sales process.

That assignment example is a simplified version. Don't hesitate to elaborate more here, because it gets the prospect thinking, "What should I know? What haven't I thought about?" For instance, in the example shared, the prospect might realize, "I haven't even thought about pool covers or heaters yet."

You'll notice the "when" came at the end, and was asked very specifically, "Will you take the time to review these two things before our appointment on Friday?" and they'll likely say "yes." Notice the final question is not "How does that sound to you?"—which renders the classic "fine" response 100% of the time (which is not a commitment, by the way).

By framing it with a yes/no question at the end, the prospect has now verbally agreed to your terms. You now have your first contract—literally—with the prospect. Creating small agreements early in the process is important because if they fulfill them at the beginning, they're much more likely to sign larger contracts later. You're training them, step by step, to form agreements with you.

Again, we stress here that it's not okay for your team to say, "It'd be great if you could give this a look before our meeting." That's not selling. It's certainly not Assignment Selling. And it's not very effective.

Following Through

Now that you've made the assignment, the next step is to confirm that they've done the homework. Here's how you might follow up:

> *"Great! I'll give you a call the morning of our appointment to confirm everything and make sure you had a chance to review the materials. This way we can hit the ground running when we meet."*

But what if they didn't do the homework?

Although this varies from company to company, our general recommendation is that you consider delaying the appointment until they've had a chance to complete it. This may seem bold, but with all the teams we've worked with, the prospects who refuse to take the time to become more educated very rarely turn into customers.

This is because if someone isn't interested in learning more to fully understand the value, then they are likely making their buying decision based on one single factor: the lowest price. And if this is the case, more often than not you'd likely lose the job anyway.

With that, let's talk implementation.

Moving Forward: Creating a Culture of Assignment Selling

If you're excited about the possibilities of Assignment Selling and its impact on your sales cycles and closing rates, you should be.

It works.

But despite the fact it works, most aren't willing to take the time to train up their sales team and make it a fundamental part of their entire sales process.

We'll discuss in detail at the end of the book putting all that you've learned into action, but understand this: **Great sales requires two main elements: great leaders and great training.**

This means that if you want Assignment Selling to work for you, your sales managers must be believers. If they are not, it will fail.

Once your managers are believers, find a few "champions" on the team who will also embrace it and are willing to immediately integrate it into their day-to-day selling.

And finally, once you have some success stories, then you can train your team on the methodology, ensuring everyone understands the *what*, *how*, and *why*—committing to long-term oversight by management and implementation by the team.

The things you've read in this chapter aren't just theoretical concepts. Let's look at how one company put these principles into action and transformed their sales results. When CSI Accounting & Payroll implemented Assignment Selling, they didn't just see modest improvements—they experienced a complete revolution in their sales process.

How CSI Accounting & Payroll Boosted Their Average Sale Price by 39.7% with Assignment Selling

When CSI Accounting & Payroll decided to revamp their sales process, they aimed to attract clients who truly understood and valued their services. They were tired of dealing with prospects interested only in quick fixes and low prices. Brian Paulson, the owner, knew it was time for a change.

Partnering with IMPACT, CSI implemented Assignment Selling with the goal to weed out bargain hunters and engage those ready for a long-term partnership.

They created a series of targeted content, including an article titled "What It's Like Working with CSI," which detailed the entire client journey—from onboarding to ongoing monthly check-ins. They also produced an 80% Video, addressing the top questions about working with CSI. These pieces were designed not just to inform, but to build trust and position CSI as a true partner.

CSI made it mandatory that prospects complete their homework before sales calls, boldly choosing not to engage with those who refused. This approach meant that by the time clients sat down with the team, they were informed, prepared, and ready to discuss how CSI could help them—while also avoiding time wasted on bad-fit, penny-pinching prospects.

The results were remarkable. In the first year of using Assignment Selling, CSI saw a 10.19% increase in their average sale price. By the second year, that increase soared to 39.7%. This wasn't just a lucky break; it was the outcome of educating clients who genuinely valued what CSI offered.

As Brian Paulson put it, "Assignment Selling didn't just change our sales process, it revolutionized it. We're closing better deals with clients who genuinely value what we offer."

CSI Accounting & Payroll's experience is a testament to the power of this approach. Assignment Selling doesn't just close deals—it builds trust, educates clients, and lays the foundation for long-term success.

19 | Building a Powerful Sales Culture Behind the Scenes: SMEs and Revenue Teams

Selling differently isn't just about customer-facing strategies like Assignment Selling or self-service tools. True transformation starts behind the scenes, where your sales culture is built and reinforced.

At the heart of this shift are two key elements: empowering your sales teams to act as SMEs and establishing a collaborative, unified "**Revenue Team**." These aren't just buzzwords—taking these two actions can radically enhance how your organization connects with buyers and drives growth.

Let's explore how building expertise and collaboration behind the scenes can create a sales culture that thrives. You'll see why these elements are essential and how they unlock the full potential of your sales efforts.

The Impact of Sales SMEs

We've established that content is essential to becoming a known and trusted brand. But here's a truth many miss: Your best content won't come from marketing alone—it comes from sales teams willing to serve as SMEs.

Why is your sales team the key to unlocking powerful insights for your business? Because they live on the front lines every single day. They're the ones hearing customer pain points firsthand, absorbing the frustrations and challenges buyers face. They're answering the same questions repeatedly, mastering how to simplify complex ideas into clear, relatable solutions. And, most importantly, they understand what actually drives buyers to take action—not just in theory, but in practice. Your sales team isn't just a resource; they're your secret weapon for connecting with your audience on a deeper level.

When your sales team actively participates in creating content, everything about your business improves—immediately and significantly. Content becomes more practical and usable in the sales process, cutting straight to what prospects need most. The stories you tell gain authenticity and relatability because they're drawn from real, frontline experiences.

The natural byproduct? Sales and marketing alignment strengthens in ways you've been striving for, and Assignment Selling becomes a seamless part of your strategy. Plus, as your sales team hones their communication skills through content, prospects feel like they know your team long before ever actually meeting. Most importantly, your collective expertise reaches more people, solidifying trust and setting your brand apart in the marketplace.

But there's an even bigger benefit: Sales team members acting as SMEs breaks down the traditional walls between sales and marketing—walls that cost companies countless opportunities every year.

Working as a Unified Revenue Team

Sales and marketing operating as separate islands is a losing strategy in today's market. Why? Because buyers are typically 80% through their journey before reaching out to sales. This means marketing handles most of the buyer's journey, yet many sales teams still believe they control the entire process.

The solution? Create a **Revenue Team.**

A Revenue Team brings together marketing, sales, and leadership to work toward one mission: making your brand the most known and trusted in your market. Think of them as the leadership team of your media company, driving content strategy and implementing Endless Customers principles throughout your organization.

What Makes an Effective Revenue Team?

Regular meetings should cover:

- Sales sharing current buyer questions and objections
- Editorial calendar planning and assignments
- Review of recently published content
- Marketing sharing performance metrics
- Addressing challenges and friction points
- Planning company-wide communications

But let's be clear—meetings alone aren't enough to drive true collaboration.

For real alignment, both sales and marketing need to fully immerse themselves in each other's worlds. Marketers should join sales calls to hear real buyer conversations firsthand and experience the questions, objections, and pain points as they happen. Sales teams, on the other hand, need to understand the trends and strategies shaping marketing so they can see the bigger picture.

And most importantly, both teams should share ownership of the entire buyer's journey, working together to create a seamless, cohesive experience that converts prospects into loyal customers.

A Word of Warning

I've seen it hundreds of times: Companies get excited about the Endless Customers strategy but think they can skip the Revenue Team piece. "Our departments work fine separately," they say. "We'll get to that integration part later."

Don't make this mistake.

Sales must fully embrace the what/how/why of Endless Customers and lock arms with marketing on the mission of becoming the most trusted brand in your market.

And marketing? Their north star should be making the sales team look great, sound great, and win more deals.

Get this right, and you'll increase 10-fold what separate departments could achieve alone. You'll also likely be "selling" very differently than anyone in your market. We've seen it happen time and time again with companies that commit to true integration.

That's the power of a Revenue Team. It's not just about working together—it's about winning together.

Be More Human
Than Others Are
Willing to Be

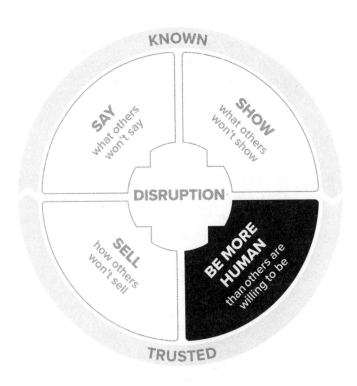

Ellie Abbott thought she was applying for a job as a furniture salesperson at La-Z-Boy Southeast. She had no idea that within months, people would walk into the store asking, "Is Ellie here today?"

You see, Ellie didn't know these people. Yet they knew her.

How? It's all because La-Z-Boy Southeast went all-in with video, "showing" what others weren't willing to show, with Ellie as one of their main subject matter experts on camera.

This perfectly illustrates the power of the first three of The 4 Pillars of a Known and Trusted Brand. When you truly say, show, and sell in ways that others won't, you naturally humanize the buying process, unlike anyone in your industry.

And there's never been a more critical time to humanize your brand than today. The rise of AI and emerging technologies is revolutionizing sales, marketing, and business.

But there's a risk: **As automation and digital tools become more sophisticated, we could lose the very thing that sets us apart—our humanity.** If we're not careful, we'll slip into a world where everything is "optimized" but nothing feels real.

But it doesn't have to be that way. Used correctly, AI and technology can make sales and marketing more human, not less.

That's why this section of the book is so important. That's also why **"be more human" is the fourth pillar of becoming a known and trusted brand.**

In this section, we want you to see what's possible when you leverage both AI and humanity. We want your customers, just like in Ellie's case, to feel like they've heard your voice, seen your face, and know *you* before they ever meet you in person. That's because being human isn't just a nice-to-have—it's becoming a fundamental differentiator and disruptor.

In this section, you'll discover how to amplify the human element of your brand while strategically using AI and technology to enhance, not replace, that essential human connection. You'll discover strategies for using AI avatars, one-to-one video, and storytelling to make your brand messaging more personal and relatable. We'll cover the importance of developing personal brands, how to ensure your content sounds more human, and why positioning your customer as the hero of your story matters.

20 | Keeping the Human Element Intact

The strength of any great buyer experience lies in connection. People don't just buy products or services; they buy into stories, relationships, and trust.

If AI and tech are used without intention, that human connection erodes. Automated responses and data-driven interactions are efficient, but they can't replace the warmth of a real conversation or the relatability of a genuine face.

But what if, instead of replacing the human touch, we used technology and AI to amplify it?

Think of AI as a tool that clears away the clutter. Let AI handle the data crunching, lead scoring, and basic follow-ups. But when it comes time to engage, bring the human touch front and center. Use that extra bandwidth to have real conversations, to reach out with empathy, and to address the nuances of human decision-making.

Personal Brands Are More Important Than Ever

As technology continues to evolve, something fascinating is happening. People are gravitating more toward personal brands than corporate brands.

Take Richard Branson, for example. People are drawn to his adventurous spirit and leadership style, not just the Virgin brand. His personality, stories, and public image spark more interest and loyalty than any ad campaign could generate. It's the human behind the brand that attracts attention.

Of course, there are many more examples than Richard Branson. Look at the following list. Who do you think gets more attention online, the person or the brand?

- Gary Vaynerchuk, VaynerMedia
- Oprah Winfrey, OWN Network
- Jeff Bezos, Amazon
- Tim Cook, Apple
- Satya Nadella, Microsoft
- Kim Kardashian, SKIMS and KKW Beauty

The numbers aren't even close.

And we're not just talking big brands like the ones listed here. Whether your company is an army of one or an army of one million, the principle here remains definitively true.

This phenomenon signals a shift. Buyers crave authenticity and a sense of connection that goes beyond logos and taglines. They want to know the people behind the brand—what they stand for, what they believe in, and what they're like when the work clothes come off. It's why leaders and teams need to be visible, relatable, and human.

The Call to Show Your Face and Share Your Soul

If you're a business leader or part of a sales team, this is your moment.

You can no longer afford to be faceless. The days of sitting behind the brand and letting it do the talking are over. If you're not willing to put yourself out there—to show your face, share your story, and let prospects see the real you—you'll very likely be left behind.

For example, at IMPACT, one of the skills we teach the sales teams we work with is one-to-one video. Instead of having them send regular, boring text-based emails (which take longer to write, are often misunderstood, and tend to be skimmed over anyway), they are trained on how to send video-based emails.

What have the results been? Consistently they hear such comments as:

> "I was so impressed that you sent me a video instead of text. No salesperson has ever done that before."
> "I love how much more personal and human your sales process is."
> "I felt like I'd already met you before we even had our first call."

The comments go on and on.

What's wild is that video-based email is incredibly cheap, often faster than text (when sending longer messages), and drives way more trust than text does. Yet most sales teams continue to do email the exact same way it was done circa 1996—that's about 30ish years of no progress.

That's sad.

Consumers want to connect with real people. They trust those who are willing to show a bit of vulnerability, and who don't hide behind corporate polish. That's why building personal brands within your business is not just smart; it's necessary. It's not enough for a prospect to trust your company; they need to trust you.

Leaders Must Lead the Charge

If you're at the helm, it starts with you. Leaders set the tone, and if you're not willing to step up and show the human side of your business, your team won't, either.

- If you're never willing to send a one-to-one video, your staff won't feel inspired to do so themselves.
- If you don't allow your marketing team to go beyond the standard "About Us" page, the world won't know your team.
- If you don't allow the sharing of behind-the-scenes stories or post videos talking about lessons you've learned, then you'll never have anyone think, "Wow, they're just like me."

Are you real, approachable, and relatable? That's what they want to know. And that's exactly the type of disruption your industry needs.

Even better, if you (as the leader) do it well, your team will naturally follow. Plus, it will even attract better employees. After all, connection is connection, in all its forms.

The Authentic 15

Speaking of authenticity, one of the frameworks we've developed at IMPACT is something we simply refer to as **The Authentic 15**—the 15 ways your brand can develop more of an authentic, "human" relationship with your audience.

We developed this list in response to the companies that had progressed well through The Big 5 and The Selling 7 (which you read about earlier in the "Say" and "Show" pillars) and had reached a place where they could take their brand to an entirely different level.

Generally, doing these 15 things takes the course of years, not days or months, to master. That said, if you're aware of them now, you can start integrating them immediately into your sales and marketing efforts.

Here is the promise: If you truly do them well and are consistent over time, they'll have a stunning impact on how the rest of your industry and market see you, changing your brand perception forever.

Here are the 15 ways you can humanize your brand in ways few others are willing to do:

1. **Tell real stories:** Share personal stories from employees, founders, or customers that highlight real experiences and challenges.
2. **Showcase employee spotlights:** On social media or on your website, highlight the diverse talents and backgrounds of employees across your company.
3. **Respond authentically on social media:** Move away from robotic responses and use authentic, personalized replies to engage with your audience, something most brands don't do. Even better, have the response come from the CEO.
4. **Create a "day in the life" series:** Develop content that shows a typical day for an employee, giving a relatable, human view of your team.

5. **Share failures and lessons learned:** Don't just highlight wins. Show setbacks and the journey to overcome them to build trust and relatability.

6. **Feature customer stories:** Showcase testimonials and real stories from customers, ideally with photos or video, to demonstrate the impact of your product or service.

7. **Use real photos, not just stock images:** Show genuine photos of your team, customers, and behind-the-scenes moments to add authenticity.

8. **Highlight social responsibility efforts:** Share your company's charitable activities, volunteer, or community initiatives with an emphasis on the people involved.

9. **Create a brand voice that's relatable:** Develop a conversational and down-to-earth brand voice that aligns with how your customers speak.

10. **Be transparent about processes:** Offer insights into how products are made or services are delivered, showing the people and decisions involved.

11. **Offer behind-the-scenes content:** Let audiences see what happens behind closed doors, whether it's product development, brainstorming sessions, or company outings.

12. **Promote real-time customer support interactions:** Showcase stories of customer support experiences where the team went above and beyond, adding a face and name to the interaction.

13. **Use humor appropriately:** Show that your brand doesn't take itself too seriously by sharing light, funny content when appropriate.

14. **Have a strong leader presence:** Encourage executives or founders to have an active, personal presence on platforms like LinkedIn, X, and TikTok.

15. **Create a podcast:** Start a podcast where team members discuss industry trends, personal experiences, or company culture.

Now, you may look at this list and say, "There's no way we could do all of that." And at first, probably not. But over time, absolutely—especially as you become more and more of a media company, as we'll discuss further in the book.

As we stated earlier, most of these will not be an initial priority. But as you continue down the path of Endless Customers and master the basics, The Authentic 15 will be your next milestone of growth and excellence.

Yale Appliance, Opes Partners, Mazzella Companies, and others you've read about have already done most of the 15 listed here, so it's very possible. It just takes a commitment to say, show, sell, and be more human in ways your competitors simply are not willing to do.

That's why it's disruptive.

It's also why few will do it.

Looking Ahead

The more you integrate humanity into your sales and marketing, the more your brand will resonate. AI can help inform, organize, and streamline, but it's your face, your voice, and your story that will stick with people. This is how you build trust and loyalty in an era where attention is fleeting and skepticism runs high.

As we move forward with the fourth pillar, we'll continue to challenge you to think differently about ways you can humanize your brand. From learning what makes a piece of content truly feel "human" to creating human-like AI avatars, this section will help you build more trust than you've ever done before.

21 | Create a More Human Website with Better Messaging

Being "more human" as a brand manifests in many different ways. One major way, often overlooked, is through the messaging of your website. Great messaging is essential for building connection, and connection is what creates a more human experience.

In this chapter, we'll explore the essential elements of crafting a customer-centric (and human) website.

Have you ever landed on a company's website and left within seconds because it was confusing?

Of course, you have. We all have.

Maybe you were greeted with a vague, corporate tagline like *"The optimal solution for your business,"* or *"The most trusted supplier since 1947."* You thought, "Optimal solution to what?" or "Supplier of what, exactly?"

If they're lucky, you might stick around for a moment, but more often you hit the "back" button and move on to their competitors.

161

Many companies waste prime real estate on their websites. They fail to accomplish the two most important things: clearly communicating what they offer, and explaining how it solves their customers' problems. They're so focused on *themselves* that they lose sight of their *buyers*—a mistake that can cost businesses thousands, if not millions, of dollars.

And even though this frustrates you as a buyer, it's likely your own website falls into the same trap.

Take a moment to pull up your website.

Yes, really—this is important.

Now put yourself in your prospective customer's shoes and try to answer these questions in less than 10 seconds:

1. What does this business do?
2. What problem do they solve?
3. How can I buy from them?

Are the answers to these questions readily available? Are they obvious to an uninformed buyer? If not, it means you have a messaging problem.

In fact, while you're on your homepage, let's do another activity. Count how many times you use the pronouns "you" or "your" versus how many times you use the words "we" or "our."

Have you counted?

Again, this is important.

What did you find?

Are you mostly using "we" and "our" language, and focusing on yourself as the hero in this story? If so, that's not good. But what *is* good is the fact that this is absolutely fixable.

And that is precisely what you'll learn in this chapter.

Ineffective Messaging Is Costing You More Than You Know

Every company has a story to tell—a narrative that explains what they offer, how they're different, and why customers should care. But here's the problem: Too often, that story is centered around the business, not the people it's meant to serve.

Think about this: 76% of visitors will leave a website if they can't quickly understand what you do or how you can help them.[1]

That's a staggering number.

It means that more than three-quarters of your potential customers could be slipping away because your message didn't hit home fast enough.

When your messaging is unclear, it's like pouring water into a leaky bucket—no matter how much effort you put into marketing and sales, it won't hold up if the core message doesn't resonate.

We're bombarded by thousands of brand messages every day—some estimates range from 6,000 to 10,000. And with the rise of AI and social media, that number is only increasing.

So how do you cut through the noise, grab attention, and create that human connection we seek?

Outside of what you've already read, the answer lies in clear, concise messaging that speaks directly to your customers' needs.

Of all the books that have ever been written on messaging, the one I believe in most comes from author Donald Miller, with his classic work *Building a StoryBrand: Clarify Your Message So Customers Will Listen*. Interestingly enough, StoryBrand is also the number-one book that is bought along with *They Ask, You Answer*, which is no surprise considering that *StoryBrand* tells you *how* to deliver your message and *They Ask, You Answer* (now, of course, *Endless Customers*) tells you *what* you should be discussing. Put the two together and you have the frameworks you need to create a website with content and messaging that is deeply rooted in the buyer—and wins their trust at an extraordinary level.

In this chapter, we'll provide an overview of the StoryBrand methodology, but for a deeper understanding, we highly recommend purchasing and reading the full book.

Reader's Resources: Need help refining your messaging? Contact our team at IMPACT. As certified StoryBrand guides, we can help you craft clear, compelling messaging that resonates with your audience and drives results.

Get Your Message Right: The Power of Story

Stories are at the heart of human communication, and they hold incredible power in branding and marketing. When your brand message follows a clear narrative, it becomes more engaging and memorable.

Donald Miller's *Building a StoryBrand* offers a simple yet powerful framework for crafting a customer-centric narrative. It's about a hero (your customer) facing a challenge and meeting a guide (your brand) who offers a clear plan, leading them to success.

Character Journey

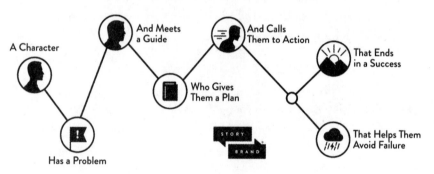

This isn't just a storytelling tactic; it's the journey your customers are already on. They're the hero, and your brand is the guide with the solution. Your messaging needs to define their problem clearly, show how you can solve it, and highlight the success they'll achieve by choosing you.

For instance, instead of simply listing features, a tech company might say, "*We know managing multiple software systems is frustrating. Our integrated platform simplifies your workflow, so you can focus on what matters most.*"

See how it's so rooted in the "problem" of the reader?

One of our clients, Neumann Monson Architects, with offices in Iowa City and Des Moines, faced this challenge. Their website was filled with impressive architectural jargon and portfolios, but it wasn't connecting with potential clients on a human-to-human level. The true value they offered— creating sustainable, innovative spaces that transform communities—was lost in technical details, leaving visitors confused and disengaged.

By adopting the StoryBrand framework, Neumann Monson shifted their messaging to focus on their clients' needs. They crafted a clear, empathetic message with a strong CTA.

Their homepage now says it all:

Enduring Architectural Solutions. Exceptional Experience.
You deserve to live, work, and play in a space that empowers you, strengthens your community, and benefits the planet. Let's help you get there.

Can you see the difference? Notice how many times the word "you" is mentioned. After all, "you" (the customer) are the hero of this story.

The result? Their website now tells a compelling story where every visitor sees themself as the hero, with Neumann Monson as the trusted guide. This shift increased client engagement and inquiries, positioning them as leaders in sustainable architecture. By making their message clear and customer-focused, they turned their website into a powerful conversion tool.

How to Craft Your Message with the StoryBrand BrandScript

The StoryBrand BrandScript consists of seven simple parts that help you utilize the power of storytelling for your brand. Here's a streamlined guide to the seven components:

1. **Identify your character:** Your customer is the hero, not your company. Define who they are and what they truly want. Be specific—don't settle for vague desires. Understand their needs in the context of your offering, and ensure your messaging highlights how you fulfill these needs better than anyone else.

2. **Determine their problem:** Great stories revolve around a problem. Articulate your customer's challenges better than they can. Address three levels: the external (tangible issue), the internal (emotions it stirs), and the philosophical (why it matters). This layered approach ensures your message is relatable and impactful.

3. **Position yourself as the guide:** Be the empathetic and authoritative guide they need. Show you understand their frustrations, and back it up with your unique expertise. Reinforce your authority with proof—testimonials, case studies, and trust-building content.

4. **Give them a plan:** Outline a simple, actionable plan that leads them from their current situation to their desired outcome. Visualize this process on your website to build trust and make the journey seem achievable.

5. **Call them to action:** Don't assume customers will act without direction. Create clear, compelling CTAs that guide them forward. Use both direct CTAs for those ready to commit and transitional CTAs for those who need more time.

6. **Help them avoid failure:** Highlight what's at stake if they don't act. This isn't fearmongering but reinforcing the consequences of inaction. Subtle reminders of missed opportunities or continued struggles can motivate action.

7. **End in success:** Show them the positive outcome of choosing your solution. Use vivid stories, testimonials, and imagery to make success tangible. Emphasize how your unique offering was key to their achievement.

These seven steps build your BrandScript—a roadmap that aligns your content with your customers' needs and positions your brand as the trusted guide. Once this is done, it's now time to turn your BrandScript into a powerful one-liner.

To do this, start with the problem, introduce your solution, and end with the success your customers will achieve. For example, a financial advisor's one-liner could be: "*We help you create a simple financial plan so you can enjoy life without worrying about your future.*"

This one-liner opens the door to meaningful conversations and ensures your message sticks, allowing you to use it over and over again across all of your content platforms.

Nail Your First Impression with a Strong Homepage Hero

Your homepage hero section is prime real estate—it's where visitors decide within seconds whether to stay or leave. Use it wisely.

Start with a clear headline that states what you do and the problem you solve. For example, if you're a basement waterproofing company, say: *"Keep Your Basement Dry and Your Home Safe from Water Damage."* Use your StoryBrand one-liner here to convey your value in seconds and then follow it with a sub-headline that expands the promise, such as, *"Expert waterproofing to keep your basement dry and mold-free, year-round."* If you have a strong differentiator, highlight it with a phrase like, *"Guaranteed for Life."*

Add a compelling CTA that stands out, like *"Get Your Free Inspection"* or *"Protect Your Home Now."* Include a high-quality image or short video that reinforces your message, such as a happy family in a dry basement or a before-and-after shot of your work.

Update the Rest of Your Homepage to Build Trust and Guide Action

Once you capture attention, the rest of your homepage should build trust and guide visitors further. Address your customers' pain points with concise, benefit-driven statements like, *"Worried about basement leaks? We've helped 1,000+ families keep their homes dry."*

Showcase your process in simple, visual steps—such as

> *"1. Inspect, 2. Design Solution, 3. Waterproof, 4. Enjoy a Dry Basement."*

This transparency builds confidence.

Incorporate testimonials and success stories to enhance credibility. Real quotes or videos from happy clients show you're trustworthy. Include a transitional CTA, like a self-assessment tool or a pricing estimator, for those not ready to commit fully.

Be Consistent with Your Messaging Across all Platforms

Your homepage sets the tone, but consistency should extend to every page of your website, and then to all of your content online. That's what's so powerful about becoming a true "guide" to your audience. No matter what platform you're on, this will help steer your language while also focusing on making your audience the hero of the message. Such is the essence of StoryBrand, and certainly Endless Customers as well.

Take Action

Clear messaging transforms your website from a digital brochure into a powerful human connection tool. When you position your customers as heroes and yourself as their guide, you build trust that drives growth.

Start with your homepage hero section, conduct your "you/we" audit, and apply the StoryBrand framework across the site and then beyond.

And remember: **Clarity trumps creativity every time.**

Your customers need to understand not just what you do, but how you'll help them succeed.

22

Connect Deeper with More "Human" Content

When was the last time you read or watched something online and immediately thought, "This isn't a human. It's AI."

It's getting all too common, isn't it?

And in those moments, when you can tell the person clearly is using AI, what is your emotion? How does it affect your feelings toward their brand?

As you know, we're in an extraordinary era of content production, where the line between AI and human-generated content blurs more each day. While we very much believe using AI is essential for efficiency and scalability moving forward, creating content that feels human—content that shows there's a real person behind it—is what creates deep human connections with audiences.

Now, this doesn't mean it *must* be created by a human. But it does mean it needs to *feel* human.

See the difference?

This chapter explores the importance of making your content look, sound, and feel more human to resonate with your audience, a subject of growing importance every day.

Why Human Content Is More Important Than Ever

Every day, your potential customers are bombarded with thousands of brand messages, and the majority sound robotic or overly polished. With AI, there's a good chance this will only get worse.

So the question is, what makes content *feel* human? There are many factors, of course, but ultimately it's the voice, the imperfections, the relatable emotions, and the stories that show there's a person behind the brand. **Human content generates trust, evokes emotion, and creates deeper connections.** This isn't just about producing content that gets clicks—it's about content that is felt, remembered, and acted upon.

As our team has been helping companies embrace AI while at the same time building a more human brand, we've found there are essentially seven main "cues" that denote a human behind the wheel.

The Seven Cues of Human Content

1. **Authentic voice and personality:** To sound human, your content must have a distinct voice. AI content often feels generic because it lacks a personal touch. Adding personality means using colloquial (informal, conversational) language, admitting what you don't know, and speaking as if you're having a real conversation. This is why if you follow me on LinkedIn (you should, by the way), you'll see I constantly use words like "dang" or "heck" or many other similar "Marcusisms"—all acting as a "cue" of my personal brand, rooted exactly in the way I talk in real life.

2. **Emotional nuance:** Human emotions are rarely singular; they're layered and often conflicting. Content that feels human captures these emotional contrasts, which make it relatable and compelling. For example, if you were a financial planning firm, you might say, *"While our clients tell us they're excited about early retirement, many admit to lying awake at night wondering if 'comfortable enough' really exists. That's why we begin every relationship with a conversation about both your dreams and your doubts."* Do you see the contrast? Very powerful.

3. **Cultural references and idioms:** Connecting with your audience means using language and examples they recognize. Phrases like *"Our new project management system is like Netflix for tasks"* use cultural touchpoints that are instantly familiar and create a shared understanding.

Analogies like *"It's like Airbnb for carbon credits"* employ industry-specific jargon and cultural cues that reinforce relevance.

4. **Imperfections and quirks:** One thing AI struggles with is purposeful imperfection, ya know? (See what I did there?) Human content isn't perfectly polished, nor should it be. Having quirks like playful self-deprecation, casual tangents, and even sentence fragments for emphasis can be incredibly effective. For example, here's what self-deprecation looks like in my world: *"I'm no Steve Jobs (heck, I can barely operate my smartphone some days), but I've learned a thing or two about innovation in my years as a pool guy."* These imperfections signal authenticity. So remember, the more perfect your content and grammar, the more distance it may actually create between you and your audience.

5. **Human experience and personal anecdotes:** Sharing real stories adds weight to your message. A line like *"We once lost a huge account because we assumed the client was on the same page with us. Turns out, we weren't even reading the same book,"* does more than tell—it shows. It demonstrates lessons learned and humanizes your brand by reflecting real-life experiences that audiences can relate to. At this point, we have a requirement with clients that *every* major piece of content should include at least one company, employee, or customer story. This also means using metaphors, idioms, or references that resonate with your audience's everyday experiences.

6. **Intuitive flow and pacing:** Content that's easy to read feels human. This involves a natural rhythm with varied sentence lengths and strategic paragraph breaks. Short, punchy sentences can emphasize key points: *"We thought we had it all figured out. We were wrong."*

   Repetition can also create emphasis: *"We innovate to solve problems. We innovate to create value. We innovate to stay ahead. But most importantly, we innovate because it's in our DNA."*

   This type of pacing gives readers space to process and, by being different, keeps them engaged.

7. **Humor and wit:** Humor is a powerful tool for making content more relatable and memorable. A line like *"Our new productivity app is so efficient, it'll give you enough free time to finally figure out what NFTs are"* adds levity and shows personality. Used wisely, humor can bridge the gap between brand and customer, making interactions feel more personal and enjoyable.

Final Thoughts: Connecting with Human Content

We realize AI is quickly getting to the point that, if you're at all skilled at using the technology, you will be able to produce content that looks, sounds, and feels completely human. However you use it, though, the human element of your brand *must* stand out. Every piece of content should signal, "There's a real person here, someone who gets you and can help."

When your content feels human, it doesn't just inform, it connects. This will always be the goal, which is why we now have to take a moment to discuss one of the most potentially controversial, and powerful developments in AI: **digital humans**.

23

The Future of Digital Humans in Customer Engagement

This chapter is a risk to write.

In fact, I debated quite a bit about including it in this book because it could be extremely outdated in a short period of time. At the same time, what you're about to read could make you think, "That's completely crazy. That's never going to happen. Marcus, you're nuts."

Whatever you feel is fine. But it has been my duty for years to tell my audiences what I see around the turn, and this is one of those subjects that feels very inevitable, despite the fact that it may be far-fetched to some. With that, let's discuss digital humans.

Imagine visiting the River Pools website and being greeted not by a chatbot, but by a digital version of me—"Digital Marcus," we'll call it—looking *exactly* as I would on a Zoom call. This digital twin turns to you and says, "Hey, I'm Digital Marcus. I want to be upfront: I'm not the real Marcus, but I carry his knowledge from years of content creation and expertise. I'm here to help you learn everything you need to know about swimming pools."

The interaction continues naturally: "We can take this conversation in two directions. I can either educate you about swimming pools—ask me anything—or I can help you get a quote for your dream pool. What would be more valuable for you right now?"

From there, visitors engage in what feels like a genuine conversation, hearing my voice, seeing my expressions, and receiving responses drawn from my entire body of published knowledge and experience.

Sound crazy?

This might feel like science fiction, but I assure you that this technology isn't just coming—it's here.

The key to successful digital avatars lies in their authenticity. They must be trained on genuine content that originates from real expertise and experience. This is precisely why creating original, authentic content is more crucial than ever. Whether through articles, videos, or podcasts, every piece of content you produce will become part of your digital avatar's knowledge base. The more authentic content you create, the more accurately your digital representative can engage with your audience.

This is also why those who have been doing Endless Customers (and previously They Ask, You Answer) for years are going to be way ahead of the game with digital humans. Again, every piece of content produced makes the avatar that much smarter and able to handle customer interactions.

Even if you choose not to create a digital twin of yourself or your team members—opting instead for a designed avatar—the principle remains the same. **This avatar needs to be trained on your company's unique insights, expertise, and voice**. This ensures that every visitor to your website receives not just information, but guidance—a human-like experience powered by AI but grounded in your real-world knowledge and expertise.

While I can't predict the exact timeline for this transformation, I'm certain of one thing: The basic, text-based chatbots we know today will soon feel as outdated as dial-up internet. The future of customer engagement will mirror real human interaction—complete with personality, nuance, and deep subject matter expertise. These won't be simple question-and-answer interfaces, but comprehensive digital guides capable of natural, flowing conversations.

Will they be perfect? Certainly not at first.

Will there be a learning curve? Yes, of course.

And because of these two "issues," many in your space will play "wait and see" instead of being the one to (as we've preached throughout this book) disrupt their industry and make waves with a more powerful customer experience.

But if you're one of the ones willing to lean into this new technology, I'd suggest you adhere to the following guidelines, guidelines that can also be used as you consider other AI technologies as well:

Immediate Transparency

Folks, as you've read everywhere else in this book, *be honest.* This should be a no-brainer: Always begin interactions by clearly identifying the digital nature of the experience. This means explicitly stating that users are engaging with an AI-powered digital human, *not* a real person. Be forthright about how the digital human was trained and what knowledge it can access. This transparency builds trust and sets appropriate expectations for the interaction.

(Note: I believe this will become a law in all countries in the future, otherwise too many consumers will be taken advantage of.)

Authentic Voice and Knowledge Base

Your digital human should only speak from verified company content and expertise, never fabricating or guessing at information. The responses should consistently reflect your brand's actual positions and policies. If the digital human is based on a specific person, it should maintain that individual's authentic speaking style and personality traits, creating a genuine extension of their presence. Along these same lines, never teach AI to lie.

Along these same lines, never teach AI to lie.

Period.

Despite the fact that some of the big AI platforms in the world were taught to lie in their early days, don't let that poor example hinder your ability to always exercise integrity moving forward.

Clear Purpose and Role Definition

Establish specific scenarios where your digital human provides the most value, such as initial consultations, product information sharing, or a preliminary quote generation. Create clear protocols for when interactions should transition to real human staff members. Don't attempt to stretch the digital human's capabilities beyond its designed purpose—this maintains credibility and ensures consistent value is delivered.

Again, going beyond the scope of capabilities needs to be a *hard stop*, every time.

Consistent Experience

Maintain unwavering consistency in your digital human's knowledge base and personality throughout all interactions. Every response should align with your company's core values and communication style. The visual presentation should remain professional and stable, creating a reliable and trustworthy presence that users can count on during each visit.

That being said, you may have different digital humans your customers can choose from, with different personalities to match what the buyer is looking for. (I know it sounds far-fetched, but it's happening.)

Ethical Boundaries

Never allow your digital human to invent information or create fictional experiences. For example, AI is very good at storytelling, meaning it could hypothetically make up stories, if asked, about a customer experience. Obviously, you don't want this to happen, ever.

Establish strict limitations around making promises or commitments that require human judgment or authority. Create clear guidelines about handling personal or sensitive information, ensuring that user trust is never compromised.

User Control and Choice

Empower users with easy options to bypass the digital human if they prefer traditional communication methods. Make alternative contact options clearly visible and accessible. Let users drive the conversation's direction and depth, ensuring they feel in control of their experience rather than constrained by it.

As always, it's all about the buyer. It's their world. Let's meet them where they are.

Quality Monitoring and Updates

Implement regular reviews of digital human interactions to ensure consistent quality and accuracy. Keep the knowledge base current as company information evolves and changes. Actively collect and respond to user feedback, using it to guide improvements and refinements to the system.

Technical Implementation

Focus on delivering reliable performance across all user devices and browsers. Prioritize quick response times and smooth interaction flows that feel natural and engaging. Develop robust backup systems and contingency plans for any technical issues that might arise.

And if it's not ready to launch, wait. This means your team may be the only one to use it and experiment with it for weeks before you roll it out to the public.

Privacy and Security

Maintain complete transparency about how user data is collected and utilized during digital human interactions. Deploy robust security measures to protect all user interactions and information.

It should go without saying, but be very careful when it comes to user data, because if there's a breach, trust in a brand can vanish immediately.

Continuous Improvement

Systematically gather and analyze interaction data to enhance response quality and relevance. Update the system based on frequently asked questions and common user challenges. Regularly expand the digital human's knowledge base with new company content and insights, ensuring it remains current and valuable. This means that as you produce new content in the future, it should immediately go into your digital human—and keep feeding it, always.

Looking Ahead

You may be saying to yourself, "Marcus, this whole time you've been talking about being more human, and now you're espousing something that is not human at all."

I'd beg to differ.

Consider this: Would someone get to know you better by talking to your digital avatar that looks like you, sounds like you, and has the knowledge of everything you've ever said online, or would they get to know you better by reading the words on your website?

And that's the thing for me. I want people to meet me in person and say, "Marcus, I feel like I already know you."

For years, I've heard that from folks who have seen me on podcasts and videos. But in the future, digital humans will be added to that list.

My advice? Don't wait to embrace this evolution.

Start building your content foundation now. The businesses that begin exploring and implementing these technologies early will set the standard for customer engagement in the digital age. The future of digital humans isn't just about technology—it's about creating genuine, scalable human connections we never dreamed possible.

Remember, it's not that we must talk to an actual human. We just want to *feel* like we're talking to a human—one who is helpful, knowledgeable, patient, and kind. With digital humans, this is very, very possible.

And with that, let's chat about the subject each of these four pillars has been leading us to: the power of disruption.

A Call
for Disruption

Now that you've uncovered The 4 Pillars of a Known and Trusted Brand, how are you feeling?

What doubts are circling in your mind?

Is there a part of you that thinks, "This seems so obvious!" yet you still wonder just how practical these concepts are to implement in your company or industry?

These feelings are not only valid, but they're also the reason why most companies that read this book will not take significant action.

Everything about Endless Customers calls for one major shift: **disruption**. Specifically, disrupting by obsessing over what buyers truly want and having the courage to deliver exactly that.

All industries are primed for disruption. Buyers are eager for it. Yet most businesses fall short—they lack the courage, vision, and strategy to make it happen.

But one truth remains: **To become the most known and trusted brand in your market, you must approach sales and marketing in a fundamentally different way than your competitors**.

24

Why Disruption Matters

Why does disruption matter so much for long-term business success? And why is it essential to your sales and marketing today?

To understand this, you first need to see how the world—and, more importantly, buyers—are changing around us.

Here are major trends your team needs to be aware of, because they help show why disruption is so essential:

- **Attention scarcity:** Consumers are flooded with thousands of marketing messages daily. Only bold, disruptive strategies break through the noise. Be that brand (for example, the famous Red Bull space jump).
- **Pattern interruption:** Brains notice the unexpected. Most marketers play it safe, but true disruption jolts attention and sticks. Break the rules you've been given and start thinking way outside the proverbial box (for example, Wendy's bold Twitter/X strategy).
- **Category commoditization:** When products blend into one, margins suffer. Disruption redefines value and builds unique advantages competitors won't see coming (for example, Warby Parker going direct to consumer with high-end, inexpensive glasses in a commoditized industry).

- **Digital acceleration:** Traditional marketing ages fast. Disruptive brands evolve where others stall (for example, Netflix shifting from DVD rentals to mail-in to digital rentals in rapid succession).
- **Shifting power:** Consumers hold more power than ever. Disruption keeps your brand relevant as control shifts from institutions to individuals (for example, Airbnb giving power to everyday homeowners over hotel chains).
- **Signal creation:** Disruption draws attention, sending signals to consumers and AI alike that your brand matters (for example, SpaceX live streaming all launches).
- **First-mover edge:** Be the first, and create competitive moats that secure your position. Keep building those moats (for example, Amazon Prime, giving unprecedented convenience to consumers).
- **Trust deficit:** Trust in institutions is at an all-time low. Authentic, transparent disruption builds real connections with skeptical audiences. (for example, Domino's famous "Oh, yes we did" campaign admitting their pizzas had been terrible).
- **Constant innovation:** Change demands reinvention. Disruption is your blueprint for continuous innovation (for example, Apple, Google, and Samsung with constant new product releases and updates).
- **Network effects:** Disruptive ideas spread fast in a connected world, boosting brand growth (for example, TikTok using user-generated content and an advanced algorithm to spread all over the world).

And there's more. The elements listed here all circle back to one core goal: building a known and trusted brand.

This is also exactly why our most successful Endless Customer clients and case studies are the ones who are constantly asking themselves the same question: *Are we disrupting?* (ourselves, our business, our industry).

When done right, disruption compels your industry to take notice. It sends an unmistakable message to both potential customers and competitors. Yet, as we've noted, most companies won't dare disrupt their industry.

Why We Resist Disruption (and Implementing Endless Customers)

Why do we resist disruption?

There are many reasons, most of them rooted in psychology. In fact, some of these have likely crossed your mind as you've read this book and thought about bringing these concepts back to your team. It's crucial to examine these now because if you don't acknowledge and address them, they'll continue to undermine your efforts.

To make these resistance points as easy as possible to understand and relate to, instead of giving you an extensive definition for each one, I'm simply going to share the most common phrase associated with each—phrases I've heard thousands of times from audiences and ones you've likely heard many times as well:

- **Loss aversion bias:** "If it ain't broke, don't fix it."
- **Organizational inertia:** "This is how we've always done it."
- **Career risk aversion:** "What if this fails and we look bad?"
- **The success paradox:** "Why change when we're already profitable?"
- **Resource allocation:** "We can't afford to experiment."
- **Cognitive biases:** "We're doing it this way, so it must be right."
- **Market myopia:** "This is how our industry works."

Overcoming Resistance and Creating a Culture of Disruption

Understanding why we resist disruption is one thing; building a culture that embraces it is another. Disruption is easy to discuss but challenging to implement.

Here's what we've found works best for organizations struggling to gain momentum:

- **Alignment workshops:** We'll cover this in more detail later, but it's crucial to ensure everyone understands the *what*, *how*, and *why* of disruption. This shared understanding is key to overcoming objections and resistance.
- **Follow a clear framework:** That's exactly what The 4 Pillars are to your business. Instead of spending all day thinking, "How do we disrupt?" it's now laid out before you.
- **Reframe risk:** Emphasize that the greatest risk is inaction. Make it clear to your team that staying stagnant is more dangerous than taking strategic risks.

- **Challenge complacency:** Self-audit constantly with the proper disruption prompts, which we'll discuss later in this chapter.
- **Make failure safe:** Create an environment where smart failures are seen as learning opportunities, not occasions for punishments.

Disrupting Beyond The 4 Pillars

As you've read about The 4 Pillars of a Known and Trusted Brand, you've seen numerous examples of how to disrupt your industry and become more known and trusted. But beyond saying, showing, selling, and being more human, there are other ways to generate ideas for industry disruption, and usually all it takes is the willingness to answer a simple question, as you'll read below.

As our clients grow and succeed in their Endless Customers journey, more and more we push them to use the following prompts to continue to drive brand awareness, trust, and new customers:

Disruption Prompt #1: Using Anger for Good

If you've spent any time in your industry, chances are you've come across common practices that frustrate or disappoint you. These frustrations can be goldmines for identifying areas ripe for disruption.

Take my experience at River Pools as an example. One thing that consistently irked us was the prevalence of misleading warranties on fiberglass pool shells. Many manufacturers included hidden clauses in their warranties, and most pool shoppers either didn't know what to look for or didn't read the fine print. This lack of transparency often led to homeowner frustration when problems arose with their pool shell.

To address this, we took an aggressive approach: We created articles and videos that explained the details of fiberglass pool warranties—the good, the bad, and the ugly. While we never singled out specific manufacturers, we did emphasize that most warranties lacked transparency and integrity.

The result? Over the next few years, many manufacturers revised their warranties to offer better consumer protection and raise industry standards.

Were these manufacturers annoyed with us for shining a light on their practices? Absolutely.

But as we mentioned earlier in this book, in the story of Steve Sheinkopf, we believed speaking up for pool owners was the right thing to do.

By tackling this issue head-on, our brand gained recognition and trust as we positioned ourselves as advocates for the consumer and drove real change (for the better) in the industry.

Now, ask yourself: *What practices in our industry make us frustrated or upset?*

Disruption Prompt #2: Setting New Industry Standards

When we first started installing fiberglass pools in 2001, we were trained to use sand as the swimming pool base and backfill material. This method was standard practice across the industry.

However, we soon discovered a significant problem: Sand settles and liquefies, which can lead to major shifting and movement.

Recognizing this flaw, we switched to using crushed stone for both the base and backfill. This change eliminated the settling issues and offered much greater stability for the swimming pool while also benefiting the homeowner long term.

Once we saw the impact of this change, we went all-in on educating the public, creating articles and videos that explained why using crushed stone was superior to sand when installing a fiberglass swimming pool.

Do you want to know what happened next? We started receiving calls from pool builders across the country, making statements like "Marcus, I've got a homeowner insisting I use stone instead of sand because they read your article online. It's causing me issues because it will cost $750 more in materials!"

My response was straightforward: "If you could install the pool in a way that better protects the homeowner's investment, even if it costs more, why wouldn't you?"

The final outcome? In 2001, about 80% of fiberglass pools in the U.S. were installed using sand. Today, around 80% are installed with stone—all because we demonstrated a better way and set a new standard.

Opportunities like this exist in every industry, often hidden in plain sight. For example, we once worked with a plastic food container manufacturer whose clients included major grocery chains worldwide. During a meeting, I asked, "Are your containers different from those of your competitors?"

Their response was immediate: "Absolutely. Ours are far more leak-proof."

"Interesting," I said. "Is there an industry standard for leak-proofing?"

"No, there isn't," they replied.

"So could we create one?" I asked.

They said yes, and just like that, we were on the path to disrupting an industry by turning a unique feature into a new standard that others would have to follow.

Once again, disruption wins.

Now, ask yourself: *What about our product, process, or method is better, different, or unique? Could we turn it into an industry standard?*

Disruption Prompt #3: Industry Awards

Disruption ideas can come from anywhere.

For instance, I was once browsing the magazine aisle in a grocery store when I noticed a magazine featuring the "*Motor Trend* Car of the Year." Immediately, a thought sparked: "Car of the Year. . .what if we had 'Pool of the Year' awards?"

At that time, we weren't yet manufacturing our own pools, which made us a basic pool dealer—similar to a small Ford dealership competing against other auto brands for business.

Inspired by *Motor Trend*, I sat down and analyzed every fiberglass pool manufacturer in the industry, assessing their models, shapes, and sizes. I then wrote an article that awarded the best models in different categories: "Best Kidney-Shaped Pool," "Best Deep-End Pool," "Best Rectangle Pool," and so on. Essentially, we were creating and giving out awards to the very manufacturers we were competing against.

The result? The article gained significant traction because no one had ever curated such an extensive list of industry-leading shapes and sizes before. Soon, some of these manufacturers (our competitors!) proudly announced on their website homepage that they had won an award for "Best Swimming Pool in Class."

Once again, disruption led to success.

So ask yourself: *What award system could exist in our industry that doesn't already?*

More Disruptive Prompts

Hopefully, you're beginning to see how powerful these prompts can be. You'll notice that they all relate back to The 4 Pillars—saying and showing what others aren't willing to.

To spark even more disruptive ideas, here are some effective prompts we've used with clients across various industries:

- What do customers in your industry most commonly complain about, and how can your company eliminate that pain point entirely?
- What is a process or aspect of service in your industry that has remained unchanged for years and could be reinvented?
- What assumptions do industry leaders make about "what customers want" that might be wrong?
- What major inconvenience do customers accept as a given in your industry?
- Where are the hidden costs or inefficiencies in your industry's traditional business model?
- What is the biggest fear or risk customers associate with buying your product or service?
- Which underutilized technology or trend could reshape your company's offerings or operations?
- What part of your customer journey has the most friction?
- What rules—written or unwritten—does your industry follow that could be broken to your advantage?
- If your company started from scratch today, how would you do things differently?
- What practices do companies in your industry hide or avoid discussing?
- What value-add could you offer that your competitors haven't even considered?
- What industry-standard metrics or key performance indicators (KPIs) could you measure or present differently to create a new benchmark?

The Path Forward

Disruption is not just a bold term—it's a company-wide mindset and a commitment to doing what others in your industry won't. It starts with a willingness to say, show, sell, and be more human than anyone else in your space. Once you do this, continue pushing forward by asking the hard questions, challenging long-held industry assumptions, and setting new standards to create entirely new benchmarks.

Since the beginning of time, it's been the rule-breakers who eventually become the rule-makers.

This is what's possible for you and your business to:

Dare to be different.
Break the industry rules.
Get known.
Win trust.
This is how you'll achieve endless customers.

Putting It All Together

Recapping the Endless Customers Frameworks

This entire book has been structured around **The 4 Pillars of a Known and Trusted Brand:**

1. **Say** what others aren't willing to say.
2. **Show** what others aren't willing to show.
3. **Sell** in a way others aren't willing to sell.
4. **Be more human** than others are willing to be.

You've learned in great detail what each of these pillars entail, and what it looks like when an organization commits to doing them really well. These pillars challenge you to think like your buyer, push boundaries, and disrupt how things have always been done in your industry.

But these pillars alone don't create results—execution does.

To achieve lasting success, there are five core areas—what we call **The 5 Components of Endless Customers**—that every organization must strengthen and optimize. These components cover the full spectrum of marketing and sales excellence:

1. **The Right Content:** Arguably the crux of it all, this component challenges you to transform your organization into a media powerhouse, consistently producing high-quality, trust-building content.
2. **The Right Website:** Your website is more than a digital storefront. It's an educational hub and an active participant in the sales process that delivers an experience the modern buyer expects.
3. **The Right Sales Activities:** This component means that you've equipped your team with a documented, content-driven process that enables seamless communication and positions them as trusted advisors.
4. **The Right Technology:** To support all sales and marketing activities, you'll need the right technology in place. This means centralizing clean, organized customer data and leveraging tools that create an exceptional experience with your brand.

5. **The Right Culture of Performance:** Success requires a commitment to growth and accountability. This component focuses on creating a company culture that values performance metrics, continuous learning, and a relentless drive for trust and transparency.

If you've grown your business to this point, you're already doing many of these components to some degree. But what comes next is refinement and improvement of each, which in turn drives your business forward and "spins the wheel" of your success.

25

Putting The 5 Components of Endless Customers into Action

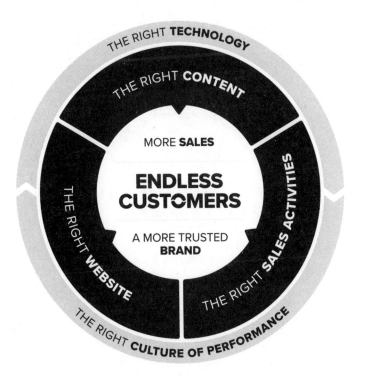

It's time to take the ideas, principles, and best practices that form the foundation of the Endless Customers System and turn them into a clear, actionable strategy. This is where theory meets execution—where the pieces come together and the system begins to take shape in your organization.

Each component is essential to building a known and trusted brand, and strengthening them is key to succeeding with Endless Customers. Let's explore what each looks like in action—these are the specific, high-impact elements that define the system.

In Chapter 26, we'll show you how to evaluate your business on these components and how systematically improving them will drive you closer to becoming the most trusted voice in your industry.

The Right Content

If there's one truth that *Endless Customers* has repeatedly emphasized, it's that content is the engine that drives everything. Buyers today are infovores—hungry for knowledge and insights that empower them to make confident buying decisions.

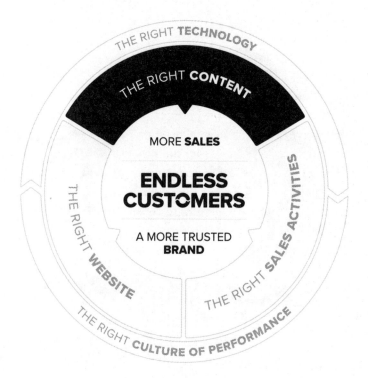

Gone are the days when prospects relied on salespeople for answers. Research now dominates the buying process, and much of it happens before a prospect ever reaches out to your team. Your content must step in to fill the gap.

Creating "The Right Content," and becoming a media company requires three key steps:

1. Commit to producing high-quality, transparent, and disruptive content.
2. Bring content production in-house.
3. Publish content on a consistent basis.

Let's take a look at each one in detail.

Step #1: Commit to Producing High-Quality, Transparent, and Disruptive Content

At the heart of becoming a media company is a commitment to the Endless Customers pillars: "Saying what others aren't willing to say" and "Showing what others aren't willing to show."

This means creating content that is helpful, transparent, and authentic— content that answers your buyers' questions and builds trust. This content pushes boundaries, takes bold risks, and is disruptive in a way that challenges industry norms and sets you apart from the competition.

Think back to the disruption prompts covered in Chapter 24. What practices in your industry make you or your buyers frustrated or upset? What award system could exist in your industry that doesn't already? This is the type of content your buyers are craving. Don't succumb to the temptation to create fluffy, top-of-the-funnel content. The content that will drive the results you're looking for takes guts to create.

Remember, the rule-breakers become the rule-makers.

The best content isn't just informative; it establishes your brand as a leader, offering buyers the confidence they need to take action. It isn't generic and it isn't produced by AI. It comes from real people within your organization.

Step #2: Bring Content Production In-House

At IMPACT, we've found that bringing content creation in-house is the single most impactful decision a company can make to succeed with

Endless Customers. The most successful companies we've worked with have *all* embraced this approach—and for good reason.

While outsourcing may seem like an easy solution, it almost always misses the mark. Why? Because outsourced content lacks the expertise, passion, and authenticity that only your team can provide. Buyers want content that reflects the real-world experience and insights of the people behind your brand, and that level of trust can't be replicated by external teams.

In-house content production also gives you the agility to create bold, disruptive ideas that resonate deeply with your audience. Outsourced support may struggle to take risks or move quickly, but your in-house team—working closely with internal SMEs—can quickly get the right type of content published and into the hands of your sales team for use.

Now, this doesn't mean you need to hire or build a massive team. But it *does* mean that someone must own the content creation process from start to finish. Without clear ownership and accountability, content production can stall, leaving your buyers without the resources they need to make informed decisions.

Typically, this means assigning someone to own (or staffing for) two specific roles:

- **A content manager:** The person responsible for writing, publishing, and optimizing content and overseeing the content strategy.
- **A videographer:** Someone focused on producing video content for articles, social media, and YouTube.

Assigning ownership of these two roles is how you build the content engine that drives your media company. To earn your buyers' trust—and ultimately their business—you need to address the hundreds, if not thousands, of questions they have. This means producing a high volume of content that answers those questions across multiple platforms and formats, creating a robust and diverse content library that meets your audience wherever they are in their journey.

So whether it's one person wearing both hats or a dedicated team, the goal should always be to have at least one full-time person fully committed to content production. Don't worry if this feels daunting or out of reach right now—we'll show you how it's possible and scalable for your organization.

If you're not familiar with what a content manager or videographer does, here are some basic guidelines as you think about how to dedicate resources to these roles.

The Content Manager

Producing great content is a full-time job, and someone has to own it.

A great content manager has the heart of a teacher, with a love of learning, writing, and communicating in all forms. They will see the value of every person on our team and put them at ease, empowering them to tell their stories to your audience.

Here are the key responsibilities and requirements for a great and successful content manager:

Responsibilities:

- Publish three or more new pieces of content per week based around The Big 5.
- Interview internal SMEs for content.
- Manage company email marketing efforts, including newsletters and automated workflows.
- Take ownership of all analytics and reporting for content marketing efforts.
- Oversee SEO efforts for website and content.
- Manage social media for community engagement and long-term content promotion.
- Produce premium content assets, including e-books, whitepapers, and webinars.
- Create landing pages and conversion opportunities for lead generation.
- Handle general website updates and enhancements, such as new pages and CTA placement.
- Leverage AI tools to speed up production processes.

Requirements:

- Impeccable writing and editorial skills.
- An understanding of common editorial style guides.
- Ability to tell great stories using words, images, or audio.

- Ability to think like an educator, intuitively understanding what the audience needs to know and how they want to consume it.
- A passion for new technology tools and usage of those tools within your own content and social media outreach.
- Clear articulation of the business goal behind the creation of a piece (or series) of content.
- Project management skills to manage editorial schedules and deadlines within corporate and ongoing campaigns.
- Familiarity with principles of marketing.
- Incredible people skills.
- Experience using AI tools to speed up the creation process.

The Videographer

To become a media company and produce impactful content like The Selling 7, someone must own your video production in-house. For most of the companies we work with, this means hiring a videographer.

Many business owners question whether a full-time videographer is necessary, and you might be asking yourself the same thing: "Does my business really need a full-time videographer? Are there really 40 hours of work per week for such a position in my niche?"

The simple answer is yes.

Showing what others aren't willing to show means that you're not only going to produce hundreds of videos per year, but you're going to build a video-first culture, and someone who knows what they're doing needs to lead the charge.

Here are the key responsibilities and requirements for a great and successful videographer:

Responsibilities:

- Produce at least two videos per week on average using The Big 5 and The Selling 7 frameworks.
- Handle all aspects of video production, including shooting, editing, and post-production, ensuring high-quality output.

- Write scripts and create storyboards to plan and visualize video content effectively.
- Work closely with the content manager to integrate video content into the broader content strategy.
- Coach and prep team members to feel comfortable and confident on camera, helping them become on-screen brand ambassadors.
- Ensure that video content is optimized for various platforms, including your website, YouTube, and social media.
- Stay updated on the latest video trends and technologies to keep your content fresh and engaging.
- Leverage AI tools to speed up production processes.

Requirements:

- Proficiency with video editing software (Adobe Premiere Pro or Final Cut Pro).
- Experience with Adobe After Effects or Motion.
- Proficiency with storyboarding, scripting, and concepting.
- Ability to conduct research and purchase needed equipment.
- Ability to operate and maintain proper levels and calibration of cameras, audio and video recorders, and other production equipment.
- Embrace of new technology like AI, augmented reality (AR), and virtual reality (VR) as it develops.
- Understanding of the importance of tracking video marketing metrics.
- Understanding of basic and advanced composition techniques.
- Understanding of the fundamentals of branding.
- Very detail-oriented and able to identify quality issues in audio and video.
- Understanding of the basics of social media and video hosting.
- Has a personal website with a portfolio, as well as a personal YouTube channel.

Reader's Resources: Looking for additional guidance on how to find, hire, onboard, and manage your content manager and videographer? Check out the EC Companion guide for plenty of resources to help you staff up these two key positions.

The Composition of an Endless Customers Team

The composition of an Endless Customers team isn't a one-size-fits-all solution.

For companies with revenues in the *$1 million to $5 million revenue range*, hiring at least one full-time role dedicated to the Endless Customers System is a smart investment. This individual often takes on a hybrid role—writing, editing, and handling video production, leveraging AI tools to amplify their impact. They need to be adaptable, capable of creating content across formats and platforms, with a special focus on short-form videos for social media.

For companies with *more than $5 million in revenue*, you're likely looking at a team of at least three to five people, including a content manager and a videographer. At the larger end, marketing teams typically expand to include three to six specialists in areas such as content, video, web management, graphic design, and data analysis. Larger businesses with multiple divisions or locations may have a content team for each division.

For companies with *less than $1 million in revenue*, the idea of having a dedicated "team" to implement the Endless Customers System may not be realistic. More often than not, the responsibility for driving the content strategy—whether it's writing articles, producing videos, or managing the website—falls on the shoulders of a key leader or even the business owner themselves. This mirrors the early days of Marcus's career as a pool guy, when he was the jack-of-all-trades, reading every book and writing every piece of content. As your business grows, you gain the ability to expand your marketing team.

Step #3: Publish and Share Content on a Consistent Basis

Your content should be published steadily across multiple formats and platforms, from articles and blogs to videos and social media posts. This means making content production an ongoing effort, not a one-time project.

We've found after years of doing this that there is a sweet spot in content production, and that's a *minimum of three pieces of content per week*.

No less.

That frequency and quantity in publishing creates necessary signals for AI to continuously recommend your content. It also helps you maintain a steady stream of fresh, new content to educate and entertain your followers until they are interested in working with you.

To stay visible and valuable, aim to publish at least three pieces of content weekly with an additional two new videos per week. This content should cover topics in The Big 5 or The Selling 7.

If you maintain this pace, you should have at least 20 pieces of content published within the first 90 days. In a year, you should be publishing over 150 pieces of content, each with written and video components. You'll also have about 100 videos published on YouTube a year.

Create a Backlog of Content

To make sure there's no break in the action, we always recommend building a backlog. Usually, this is 5–10 pieces of content, already scheduled to be released, at all times, while you're working on content.

Your content should be prepared far enough in advance that if anyone takes a sick day, is on vacation, or something comes up, your content publication doesn't come to a screeching halt. This is what it looks like to think like a publisher and strive to be a media company.

Stick to Your Publishing Schedule

Once you start publishing, it's important that you maintain a consistent publishing schedule. Algorithms reward consistent publishing, too, but there's something much more powerful than an algorithm expecting content from you: your buyers. Your audience will get used to when you publish new content, when to expect your newsletter, or when your next podcast or YouTube episode comes out.

Of course, you still have the flexibility to move stuff around and be reactive when you want to address something timely. If something happens and you want to publish a specific piece of content early, or possibly post-pone a piece of content until later, you can and should do that.

Expand to Other Channels

While written content often serves as the foundation of a strong content strategy, it's just the beginning. Companies that succeed with the Endless Customers System quickly realize the power of diversifying their content formats and expanding to other platforms.

Video, as we've discussed in Section 3, is the natural next step. You-Tube, the second-largest search engine in the world, is a goldmine for building trust, showcasing expertise, and connecting with your audience on their terms. As YouTube continues to grow in importance, businesses that fail to prioritize this channel risk being left behind.

Beyond YouTube, podcasts and other episodic content help deepen audience relationships. Podcasts allow you to share long-form insights, tell compelling stories, and create a sense of intimacy that other mediums can't match. They also provide a convenient way for buyers to engage with your brand while commuting, exercising, or multitasking.

Don't forget the power of repurposing. A single video can be trans-formed into multiple pieces of short-form content for social media. Plat-forms like Instagram, TikTok, and LinkedIn are perfect for bite-sized, engaging clips that draw attention and spark interest. By adapting your con-tent for these formats, you can expand your reach and keep your audience engaged no matter where they spend their time.

Utilize Paid Media

Many businesses wonder how or if paid media has a place in Endless Customers. The short answer is yes—but only if you have the right content and strategy in place.

Paid advertising isn't a quick fix or a magic bullet to instantly drive sales. Businesses often throw money at ads without the right strategy, expecting instant results, only to be disappointed. When ads "don't work," it's rarely the platform's fault. More often, the issue lies in the strategy. Without high-quality content to drive visitors to, paid campaigns can fall flat. Ads are a tool to *amplify* what's already working—not a substitute for a strong foundation.

You can't simply flip a switch and expect ads to deliver results overnight. Building your audience and gathering the insights needed to target the right buyers takes time. That's why we recommend focusing first on creating a library of high-quality, trust-building content. Once your content strategy is running smoothly, paid media can help you extend your reach, driving additional views, engagement, and traffic to your site or YouTube channel.

Reader's Resource: Check out the EC Companion Guide for our latest recommendations for accelerating your Endless Customers content through paid ads.

Make It a Company-Wide Initiative

The marketing team is responsible for publishing a regular cadence of content designed to generate leads and drive results. But don't make the mistake of thinking this is solely a marketing play. Endless Customers is just as much a sales initiative. At the end of the day, what we're aiming to do is sell and retain endless customers.

Yes, you need to put someone from marketing in charge, but they can't do it alone. Becoming the most known and trusted brand in your market takes everyone, especially leadership, your sales team, and all other customer-facing employees.

Take the example of Thad Barnette at Sheffield Metals. With no prior experience in metal roofing, Thad joined the company in 2018 to spearhead a video strategy that positioned Sheffield as a leader in metal roofing expertise.

Thad had a great personality and a knack for video, but wasn't a roofer by trade and knew nothing about the technical aspects of metal roofing. But that was the genius behind it. Instead of trying to act like an expert from day one, he put himself in the shoes of the customer—interviewing members of the sales team and contractors in the field, seeking answers to the questions he knew buyers were asking. His style was approachable, educational, and authentic. Viewers saw someone who was genuinely curious, just like they were, and that built a strong connection.

His efforts led to the creation of more than 500 videos on the Metal Roofing Channel on YouTube, garnering millions of views and generating more than 60 qualified leads per week. This content didn't just build trust—it drove more than $20 million in sales within a few years, transforming Sheffield's business and establishing Thad as a trusted face of the brand.

This success wasn't Thad's alone—it was a team effort. The deep product knowledge came from Sheffield's employees, and their collaboration turned content into trust and trust into revenue. This story illustrates the power of an in-house content strategy: It's not just about creating content, but about ensuring it authentically captures the expertise and passion of your team. When content creation becomes a company-wide initiative, the results can be extraordinary, building trust, driving revenue, and elevating your brand as a market leader.

Thad was accountable for getting the right content out the door on a consistent basis, but none of it would've happened without the expertise and support of others in the company. The technical knowledge, the field experience—that didn't come from Thad. It came from the SMEs he worked with, and that collaboration is what made their content so powerful.

When the sales team actively participates in the content creation process, the content is better. Your sales team is the one closest to your customers. They hear their pains, frustrations, and objections firsthand. They know the questions prospects are asking and exactly how to answer them. In fact, they are probably answering the same questions, the same way, every time, stated and communicated in a way that the prospect understands, resolving their concerns.

But marketing needs the sales team—their knowledge is pure gold for content creation, offering the fastest path to producing content that truly connects with your audience. And when they publish that piece of SME-inspired content, that's just the beginning.

To maximize its value, your sales team must actively use this content to engage prospects and close deals more efficiently. This requires that marketing make it a habit to share new content with your sales team regularly, equipping them with resources they can send directly to prospects to answer questions, address objections, and build trust throughout the buyer's journey.

The Right Website

With 80% of the buying process happening before a prospect even speaks to sales, it's clear your website has to do the heavy lifting.

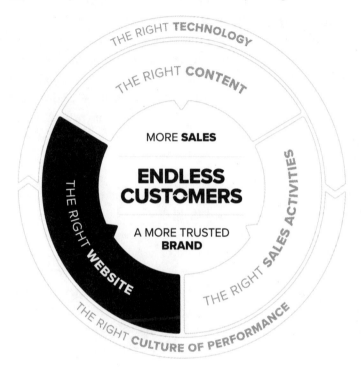

Achieving "The Right Website" requires six key steps:

1. Get your website ready for Endless Customers.
2. Hone your website's messaging.
3. Simplify your navigation.
4. Launch a "Learning Center."
5. Integrate self-service tools.
6. Continually optimize and improve.

Step #1: Get Your Website Ready for Endless Customers

For the same reasons you need to bring content production in-house, your website must also be managed with agility and adaptability. It should support your content and sales strategies, enabling your team to make updates quickly and efficiently.

At a minimum, your team should be able to publish content regularly, update navigation with ease, add and modify pages, and effectively capture and manage lead information. The team needs access to your content management system (CMS) and the knowledge to use it properly to make these updates.

We're not saying you need to fully redesign your website. In fact, while the advice you'll typically get from marketing agencies is to start with a full website redesign, we do not recommend this. Start with small updates, prioritize publishing content, and save the major overhaul for later, if it's even needed at all.

Someone on your team should know how to analyze your website for major technical issues that may be hindering its performance, such as slow load times, poor mobile performance, or security vulnerabilities. These problems frustrate visitors and block your website from getting found by search engines and AI tools.

You'll also need the right tools to monitor and understand user behavior; otherwise, making informed decisions will be impossible. At a minimum, you need to add basic analytics tools like Google Analytics. Tools like this give you real-time insights into visitor behavior, helping you refine your strategy and make data-driven decisions about changes to your website.

Finally, as technology evolves, your website must also adapt to meet modern buyer expectations. In an AI-first world, integrating tools like chatbots, predictive content suggestions, and advanced analytics can help your site provide a more personalized and efficient user experience. By staying ahead of these trends and leveraging the latest tools, you'll ensure your website continues to meet the needs of today's buyers while remaining a central driver of business growth.

Reader's Resources: Need help building and learning how to manage your website? Contact the team at IMPACT. We coach and train businesses on how to own their website and turn it into their most powerful salesperson.

Step #2: Hone Your Website's Messaging

When refining your website messaging, remember the core StoryBrand principles you learned in Chapter 21: Your customer is the hero, and your brand is the guide.

Start by crafting a clear, compelling message that passes the grunt test. In other words, a visitor should instantly understand what you do, how you make their life better, and what steps they need to take next. If your homepage or landing pages don't answer these questions within a few seconds, your message isn't hitting the mark.

You need to test and refine your message, and your sales team plays an important role here. They're on the front lines, speaking directly with prospects, and will know right away if your website is delivering or falling flat. If they start conversations with people who are confused about your offer or need more explanation, that's a sign your messaging needs tweaking. Use this feedback to adjust and simplify your content, focusing on what matters most to your target audience.

Treat your website messaging as a living, evolving part of your strategy, and understand that you may not get it right on the first or second try. Continuously collect input from your sales team, A/B test variations, and analyze engagement data.

When you do get it right, you'll notice a shift—your sales conversations will start further along because prospects already understand your value. That's the power of nailing your website messaging.

Step #3: Simplify Your Navigation

Your visitors should never struggle to find what they're looking for on your website. With so much content on your site, organizing it in a clear and accessible way should be a top priority.

In our experience, when companies create a simple, clear navigation, they see a noticeable increase in user engagement. A well-structured site not only makes it easier for visitors to find valuable content but also builds trust by offering a seamless user experience.

Start with the basics. Your navigation should include the most important elements of your website—links to your product or service pages, your Learning Center (which we explain in the next step), pricing information, and a clear way to contact you. Don't clutter your main navigation with internal information like "about us" pages, which can be relocated to the footer. You can also eliminate outdated elements, like the "home" link, because most visitors know they can click on your logo to return to the homepage.

Next, organize your navigation in the order that aligns with the buyer's journey. For example, your product/service page(s) should appear on the left, where users naturally begin exploring. Pricing information, a critical step in decision-making, should be further to the right.

Speaking of pricing—yes, you need to include a link to find pricing information within your website's navigation. Revisit Chapter 5 for a reminder of how to create the "Perfect Pricing Page." This may look like content and videos addressing cost, a pricing estimator self-service tool, or even both.

Don't leave an interested visitor hanging. Make it incredibly easy to take the next step and contact you when they're ready. Whether it's a form to fill out or another way to connect, the action you want them to take (your primary CTA) should be clearly visible in your navigation to guide visitors smoothly through the buyer's journey.

Remember, there's no room for fluff in your main navigation. Anything that doesn't directly contribute to the buyer's journey should be moved to the footer—or removed altogether.

Step #4: Launch a Learning Center

Just like a great salesperson anticipates the questions a buyer will ask, your website must do the same. It should quickly and clearly deliver the information your potential customers need. That's where a Learning Center comes in.

If you've been wondering, "Where does all this content go?" the answer is: your Learning Center.

A **Learning Center** is a dedicated section of your website where all your best content is organized, easy to access, and designed to educate your prospects. Unlike a typical blog, it's more than just a chronological list of posts. It's a strategically structured hub that brings together articles, videos, podcasts, webinars, guides, and tools—giving visitors exactly what they need based on their stage in the buying process.

It's also a powerful tool for your sales team. To close more deals faster, we need our salespeople spending less time educating and more time selling.

With all your best content in one place, easily searchable by any question a prospect has, your sales team can quickly find relevant content to easily share with prospects. This process, known as Assignment Selling (which we discussed in Chapter 18), saves them hours they would have otherwise spent on explaining and teaching.

A great Learning Center should be four things:

1. Searchable
2. Segmentable
3. Easy to use
4. Located in the navigation

A great example of a Learning Center that does all of this well is from a company called AQUILA, a commercial real estate company based in Austin, Texas.

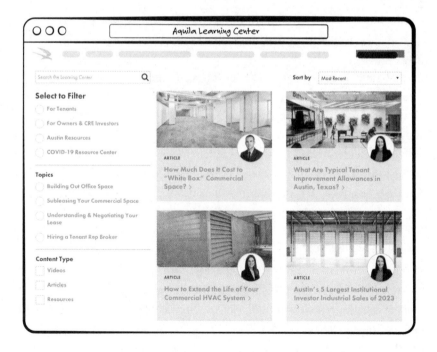

Searchable: First, you'll see that the Learning Center has a search bar located right at the top. It's easy to find and use.

Segmentable: Their Learning Center content can be filtered by content type, topic, and even audience type. They have filters for tenants, owners, investors, and more. You also have the option to sort content by most recent or most popular.

Easy to use: The Learning Center is intuitively built, with checkboxes for filters where you can select multiple options and radio buttons for filters where you can only choose one option at a time. The content displayed has easy-to-read titles and regardless of exactly where you click, you'll be taken to the piece of content.

Located in the navigation: AQUILA's Learning Center is located in their top navigation and stays there no matter where you navigate on the website.

Step #5: Integrate Self-Service Tools

As discussed in Chapter 17, self-service tools are often the quickest way to increase conversions, build a contact database, and generate sales-ready leads.

By implementing self-service tools you can seamlessly guide buyers through their journey while capturing valuable data. Keep it simple, focus on the core needs of your audience, and use these tools to both build trust and accelerate the decision-making process.

Start by identifying the key areas where visitors most often seek assistance. Do they need help understanding pricing? Use a pricing calculator. Are they unsure which product fits their needs? A product configurator or quiz can guide them to the best option. Refer back to Chapter 17 or the EC Companion Guide if you're looking for more examples.

Once you've identified the tool(s) you want to create, you can choose between custom-built and out-of-the-box tools based on your needs and resources. While custom tools are ideal for businesses with complex or specialized needs, prebuilt solutions can be an effective choice for companies looking to launch a tool quickly.

Position them prominently on your site and make sure they are simple to navigate, reducing any friction.

Step #6: Continually Optimize and Improve

As you work to create a website that captures your market's attention and fuels sales opportunities like no other in your space, keep in mind that a website is never truly "done."

Publishing new content multiple times a week is important, but the real impact comes from tracking and optimizing how that content performs. Are your prospects engaging with it? How are they navigating your site, and where are they converting—or dropping off? Just like a top salesperson who constantly reviews and adjusts their pitch, your website demands the same level of attention.

Ask yourself: If we refined the messaging on this page or moved this section higher up, would it improve the buyer's journey and boost our site metrics? What about adding a self-service tool—would that make the experience more seamless? When you view your site on mobile, does anything feel clunky or out of place? And are there any technical issues in the background hurting your site's performance that need addressing?

Make it a priority to evaluate and take action every month. Every improvement brings your website closer to becoming the most trusted and best-performing website in your market.

Reader's Resources: Looking for additional guidance on how to manage your Endless Customers website? Check out the EC Companion guide for plenty of resources to help you refine and optimize your website for the modern buyer.

The Right Sales Activities

As you now know, Endless Customers is a sales-first strategy. When the sales and marketing teams are working together closely to create content for the sales process, there should be an immediate impact on sales. This is how you will be able to sell in a way others are not willing to sell. So how do you do it?

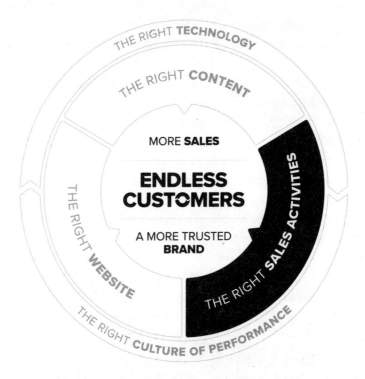

Implementing "The Right Sales Activities" requires four key steps:

1. Sales team participates in content creation.
2. Sales process is documented and followed consistently.
3. Integrate Assignment Selling into your sales process.
4. Create a sales culture of continuous improvement.

Step #1: Sales Team Participates in Content Creation

Your best content will come from insights shared by your sales team. Those on the front lines interacting with buyers will contribute ideas for content that helps move deals to the finish line. They'll know how to answer questions the way a buyer would understand.

When the sales team actively participates in the content creation process, the content is more closely tied to actual sales conversations, appealing to prospects, and likely to be used by the sales team in Assignment Selling.

When the sales team is visible and active in content efforts, prospects start requesting to work with them by name, like how customers walk into a La-Z-Boy store asking to work specifically with Ellie.

This does mean that your sales team must be willing to be on camera and you need to make sure they're trained to appear confident and comfortable in their videos. For help with this, revisit the SIMPLE On-Camera Performance Checklist from Chapter 16.

Beyond working with marketing to create video content, your sales team should be creating one-to-one videos to use in the sales process. Don't allow your sales team to be outdated and live in the past with plain old text-based emails. Make sure they're trained to connect with prospects through videos they can send directly in emails. These videos are faster to create than written emails and, as you saw in Chapter 20, people are consistently impressed when they receive a video email.

Remember, consumers want to connect with people. Encourage your sales team to show a little humanity to build trust as they get started with a new prospect or take a prospect to the finish line.

Reader's Resources: Want more help with training your team to be effective on camera? Check out the EC Companion Guide for tips and educational resources.

Step #2: Sales Process Is Documented and Followed Consistently

Remember, as outlined in Chapter 18, your sales process must be clearly documented, systematic, and repeatable. It should guide your sales team through each stage of converting a prospect into a customer. It should map out the specific actions, milestones, and requirements that must be met at each stage, ensuring consistency in how deals progress and how the sales team engages with prospects.

When it comes to documenting your sales process, less is often more. Think about it like a pilot's checklist—focused on the key steps that can't be missed, without bogging down in unnecessary details. Your goal isn't to create a manual that covers every single action a seller might take. Instead, hone in on the key stages and actions that drive the sale forward.

But remember, this isn't a one-and-done exercise. It needs to be revisited, revised, and optimized as your business evolves and as you learn more about what works and what doesn't. The most successful sales teams are the ones that constantly refine their process, keeping it sharp and relevant to the buyer's needs and the realities of the market.

Step #3: Integrate Assignment Selling into Your Sales Process

As Marcus introduced in Chapter 18, Assignment Selling is the practice of requiring prospects to consume specific educational content before sales conversations to improve close rates and reduce sales cycles.

Once you have your sales process defined, the next step to prepare your team for success with Assignment Selling is to map helpful, educational content to each step in the sales process.

Your team needs to know *exactly* what content to use and when to use it to be successful. Early-stage prospects might benefit from introductory articles or videos that provide a broad overview, while those closer to a decision may require detailed case studies or product comparisons. It's vital that you take the time to outline your sales process and map content to each stage so your entire sales team is aligned on which content to use when.

Step #4: Create a Sales Culture of Continuous Improvement

Now that your sales process and content is documented, the real work starts. Your team needs to use it consistently—and that starts with training. Your process is only as strong as your team's ability to follow it, so everyone needs to be on the same page from day one.

Also as mentioned in Chapter 18, you need to provide your sales team with thorough training so they fully understand the process and can confidently apply it. Beyond that, they must also know where to find content and when to use it in the sales process. They should have practiced with their Assignment Selling script and should be recording and regularly reviewing their sales calls.

They should practice through role-play activities to refine their approach and build confidence. Sales leaders should offer regular feedback to maintain consistency and keep everyone aligned with the process.

Finally, you should continuously update the sales process you documented based on your sales team's experience using it.

The Right Technology

To support your sales and marketing efforts effectively, you need the right tools and systems in place. Technology provides the foundation for your team to work efficiently, stay aligned, and deliver a seamless buyer experience. By centralizing customer data, automating repetitive tasks, and integrating tools like chatbots and predictive analytics, the right technology allows your team to focus on what matters most: building trust and driving results.

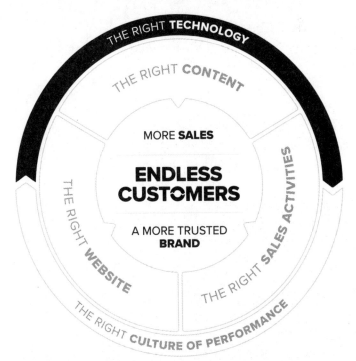

Adopting "The Right Technology" involves five key activities:

1. Centralize your customer data with a CRM.
2. Train for proper CRM usage and maintain accountability.
3. Set AI guidelines for your company.
4. Train your team on AI.
5. Create a culture of AI and technology experimentation.

Step #1: Centralize Your Customer Data with a CRM

A customer relationship management system (CRM) is essential for breaking down silos and creating a seamless experience for both your team and your customers. By centralizing accurate customer data, everyone—from sales and marketing to customer service—has access to the same information, enabling faster, more informed decision-making.

A CRM gives leaders real-time visibility into deals, marketing campaigns, and customer interactions. Sales teams can find critical information without hunting through emails. Marketing can track which campaigns are driving revenue, and customer service can access full interaction histories to provide smooth, personalized support.

The result? A more efficient team and a better customer experience.

A great CRM doesn't just store contact details. It captures every touchpoint in the buyer's journey—from the content they've read to the videos they've watched and interactions with your team. This holistic view helps you understand their needs and guide them toward a purchase with confidence.

The best CRMs perform five key functions: centralize customer data, track the sales pipeline, connect marketing activities to revenue, enforce structure and processes, and improve efficiency with automation and AI.

HubSpot stands out as an industry-leading CRM that checks all these boxes. It integrates marketing, sales, and service tools into one seamless platform, and is user-friendly, scalable, and heavily invested in AI features. HubSpot's commitment to constant innovation and ease of use makes it a popular choice for companies serious about growing with an organized, data-driven approach.

Reader's Resources: If your CRM doesn't perform the way your business needs it to, consider switching to a system that does. We recommend HubSpot to all of our clients. It's the only platform that lets you track actual sales revenue back to specific content on your website. Scan the QR code to see for yourself.

IMPACT may receive compensation from HubSpot for signups. This in no way affects IMPACT's recommendation of HubSpot.

Step #2: Train for Proper CRM Usage and Maintain Accountability

A CRM is only as effective as the data entered into it, and that's where many companies falter. Proper usage doesn't happen by chance—it requires a dedicated effort to train your team and hold them accountable.

Far too often, businesses invest in a CRM but neglect the ongoing work required to ensure data quality. This leads to records full of inaccuracies, missing information, and outdated entries, making it hard to trust the system or use it effectively.

The consequences of poor data hygiene are severe.

Inaccurate or incomplete records lead to misinformed decisions, wasted resources, and frustrated team members. If marketing is basing campaigns on outdated data, or if sales reps are making calls without knowing a lead's full history, everyone suffers. The lack of training and accountability is the main culprit behind these issues.

That's why the mantra should be: *If it's not in the CRM, it didn't happen.* Every interaction must be logged. Every note must be recorded. And it starts with leadership setting the tone for the rest of the organization.

Holding people accountable doesn't just mean monitoring CRM usage—it means explaining why it's so important. Training should emphasize that the CRM isn't just an admin task; it's a vital tool for improving performance and collaboration. Everyone needs to see the bigger picture: using the CRM properly benefits the entire company and enhances the customer experience.

Step #3: Set AI Guidelines for Your Company

The use of AI in sales and marketing is no longer optional.

Throughout the book, we've discussed the immense potential AI holds to transform your business. AI tools automate routine tasks, enrich data, and provide actionable insights, freeing up your team to focus on what truly matters: building relationships and closing deals.

However, to be successful with AI, you need to set guardrails for your team.

Establishing clear guidelines for AI usage is crucial to avoid confusion and ensure that AI-driven tools are used ethically and effectively. Set boundaries around data use, privacy, and the scope of automation. Make sure that everyone knows the rules for handling sensitive customer information and that any AI-driven processes comply with industry standards. These guidelines protect your company while allowing your team to maximize the value AI offers.

We created what we call our S.A.F.E.T.Y. guidelines, and for most companies we work with, it's a great starting point for your guidelines, too. You can certainly take this, adopt it, and make it work for your organization.

AI S.A.F.E.T.Y.

S ecure

A ssistive, not autonomous

F act-checked

E xperimental

T ransparent

Y our expertise matters

We say that any AI experimentation needs to be:

- **Secure:** We must keep our (and our clients') data safe. Before using any tool, check the data security levels and act accordingly. If you're not sure, don't risk it.
- **Assistive, not autonomous:** AI is a helper, not a team member. A human must always be in the loop. We are accountable for what AI does, and our oversight is vital.
- **Fact-checked:** We would never blindly publish anything AI produces. We check everything.
- **Experimental:** AI has the potential to enhance the quality of our work and increase our output. We need to explore its capabilities through experimentation to see how.
- **Transparent:** Our use of AI is not a secret. We should be transparent with coworkers, supervisors, clients, and our audience, including proper citation of sources.
- **Your expertise matters:** AI can amplify your creativity and speed up your repetitive tasks. None of this is possible without your expertise. Let AI multiply your impact for the greater benefit of the organization.

These guidelines are broad enough to cover big concerns. Just like everything else, encourage your people to use their best judgment. When implemented correctly, guidelines don't hinder experimentation, they facilitate it.

We recommend you take what we have here, use them as a starting point, and make them your own. While we're presenting these as guidelines, we fully understand that at your company or in your industry, you may require more stringent and definitive policies to address specific risks and compliance requirements.

Additionally, outline who is responsible for monitoring AI's impact on your workflows and who employees should approach with questions or suggestions. This accountability ensures that AI is being used to its fullest potential while keeping your business operations secure and efficient.

Step #4: Train Your Team on AI

When you get started, some members of your team will be excited to learn to use AI, while others will be hesitant and skeptical. Some may even be scared it will take their jobs. If you're like most organizations, it's likely you'll have employees who are all over this spectrum.

This is exactly why AI education should be a priority. It's not enough for a few tech-savvy employees to understand the potential of AI. Everyone in the organization must know the role AI plays in your strategy and how it impacts their work.

Start with an overview of your company's stance on AI, emphasizing why it's essential and what benefits it brings. Make learning accessible through workshops, webinars, or an internal communication channel dedicated to sharing AI insights. The goal is to demystify AI and show your team how it simplifies their work.

Step #5: Create a Culture of AI and Technology Experimentation

Once you've set clear guidelines and gotten your team familiar with the capabilities of AI, experimentation must be part of everyone's job description.

AI shouldn't be a niche tool for a select few—it should be embedded into your company culture, with all team members encouraged to innovate and explore new ways of working. This means creating an environment where risk-taking is celebrated, and failure is treated as a learning opportunity.

Encourage your team to think creatively about how AI can enhance your marketing, sales, and service efforts. Provide structured opportunities for experimentation, such as hackathons or dedicated time for employees to test out new tools and processes. Recognize and reward those who take the initiative to push boundaries, even if their experiments don't always succeed.

When AI and technology experimentation become a norm, your company stays agile and ahead of the competition. Remember, the companies that win are those that embrace discomfort, adapt to change, and continuously find ways to improve.

The Right Culture of Performance

Endless Customers only works if you fully embrace it as a culture change within your organization. The way your company operates, and how you think collectively as a team, will change.

Like any other company priority, Endless Customers only works when leadership makes it a company priority. It starts with leadership investing the right amount of time and resources needed to make it a success. They also must hold people accountable, celebrate wins, and regularly reinforce the principles.

The people at your organization must have a desire to learn and experiment. As soon as this book is published, changes will occur—new platforms and new technologies will arise—and the best companies experiment, learn from it, and embrace it.

You will never get ahead by waiting for others to do something first.

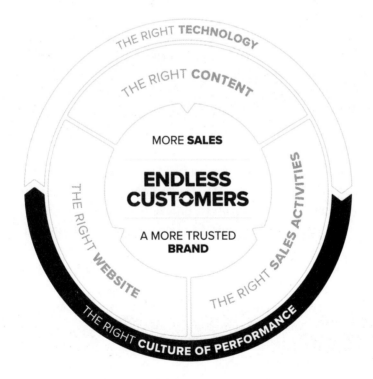

Bringing "The Right Culture of Performance" into your organization happens in four steps:

1. Get buy-in from leadership.
2. Align your entire organization with Alignment Day.
3. Hold Quarterly Planning Sessions.
4. Repeat Alignment Day annually.

Step #1: Get Buy-In from Leadership

Everything begins with leadership. If you're not willing to take risks, your company won't, either. The tone is set at the top, and it's your responsibility to lead the charge.

Fear is the biggest reason leaders hold back.

Fear of failure. Fear of rocking the boat. Fear of doing something that your competitors—or worse, your customers—might not like.

But that fear is the very thing keeping you stagnant.

If you want to truly become the most known and trusted brand in your market, you have to overcome any fear standing in your way from taking bold actions. Your team is looking to you to set the example.

It starts with you.

If you're the CEO or business owner and you're already reading this book, then you've checked the box on this step. But if you have a business partner or another key decision-maker who needs to be on board, it's important that they catch the vision as well. Major business decisions require alignment, and this is no different. To move forward effectively, they need to fully understand the potential of the Endless Customers System.

Now, what if you're not the CEO or business owner, but you're someone else on the team who sees the potential of this system and wants to introduce it to leadership? You might be asking yourself, "How do I pitch this to my boss?"

Our recommendation: Don't.

Instead of trying to convince them yourself, encourage them to engage directly with the material. Let the system speak for itself.

So how do you get leadership bought in? In our experience, two actions have proven to be the most effective at helping leadership fully grasp and get excited about the power of Endless Customers:

1. **Read *Endless Customers*:** The book immerses readers in The 4 Pillars of a Known and Trusted Brand, The 5 Components of Endless Customers, and the frameworks that help implement the strategy. It explains the *what*, *why*, and *how* of the system in a way that resonates with leaders, using real-world examples that bring the principles and strategies to life. It's the best way to understand how the system works and visualize the transformation in a company.

2. **Attend an Endless Customers event or talk:** Another powerful way to catch the vision of the Endless Customers System is by attending a live event or talk. These experiences are always rooted in the fundamentals of the system, ensuring attendees gain a solid understanding of its core principles while learning the most up-to-date applications. Plus, it gives attendees a chance to connect with like-minded leaders who are already applying the system or are eager to adopt it, giving valuable insights and inspiration.

By taking one or both of these actions, you'll give your leadership team the chance to see firsthand why so many businesses have embraced this system to build trust, drive transparency, and achieve extraordinary results. This is how you will stay focused on being a disruptor and living the pillars. That means risk taking, learning, and experimentation.

You can't play it safe.

Once leadership is on board with the Endless Customers System, the path forward becomes much easier. Your commitment will create the momentum needed for the entire organization to get on board and begin the transformation. Leadership sets the tone for everything that follows—and when the leadership team is fully invested, the rest of the organization will follow suit.

Getting everyone on the same page starts with an Alignment Day.

Step #2: Align Your Entire Organization with Alignment Day

To launch Endless Customers successfully, your entire organization—sales team, marketing team, leadership team, and anyone else who interacts with customers—needs to rally around a single, unified customer acquisition strategy. Everyone must be on the same page and fully committed to moving in the same direction.

The solution? **Alignment Day.**

Alignment Day is a focused, three-hour training session designed to unify your team around the principles of Endless Customers. During this time, we break down barriers, clarify the strategy, and get everyone pulling together toward a shared vision for customer acquisition.

What's covered during Alignment Day:

1. **How buyers have changed:** Explore the modern buying journey and how much of it happens before prospects ever reach out. Highlight the shift in buyer expectations and the role your team must play.
2. **The 4 Pillars of a Known and Trusted Brand:** Break down the core principles that differentiate businesses and discuss the practical applications for each pillar across sales and marketing.
3. **Brainstorming topics and strategies:** Generate ideas and strategies to bring The 4 Pillars to life through your content, marketing, and sales efforts.
4. **Define roles and responsibilities:** Every participant will leave with a clear understanding of how Endless Customers impacts their role, what's required of them to execute effectively, and how their efforts contribute to the success of the whole team.

By the end of Alignment Day, your team will not only understand the "why" behind Endless Customers but also the "how." Everyone will know their role in making the strategy work—and, most importantly, they'll be inspired to own it.

It's tempting to see this as a marketing effort alone or to leave out parts of the sales team. Don't. When your entire customer-facing organization isn't involved, gaps form, the strategy falls apart, and results suffer.

There's an old saying: "You can be a prophet to the world, but no one is going to listen to you in your own hometown." As a leader, you know this better than anyone. Your team hears from you all the time—on strategy calls, in team meetings, during one-on-ones. That constant exposure, while valuable, has an unintended side effect: Your message, especially when presenting new ideas, doesn't always hit the way you intend it to.

It's not your fault. It's human nature. Familiarity dulls the impact.

When you talk about change or a bold new strategy like the Endless Customers System, your team might nod along, but deep down, they may not feel the urgency or importance.

This is where an outside voice makes all the difference.

When an Endless Customers Certified Coach facilitates Alignment Day, they bring fresh energy and an unbiased perspective, cutting through the noise of daily routines. They'll deliver the same key messages you would—but in a way that resonates differently, precisely because it's coming from someone outside the organization.

As one leader put it after their Alignment Day: "They just said what I've been saying for months, and the team acted like it was brand new. But you know what? It worked." And that's the point. It's not about who gets the credit—it's about getting your team to rally behind a shared vision.

We'll talk more about the role of a Certified Coach and how they can help accelerate your journey mastering the Endless Customers System in Chapter 27.

Skipping an Alignment Day can be costly.

Take it from one of our clients, Patrick Accounting, who struggled to implement parts of the strategy on their own. Without an Alignment Day, their sales and marketing teams worked in silos, leading to miscommunication and frustration.

Realizing they were stuck, Matt Patrick and Mike Schaeffer reached out to IMPACT for help. They discovered that without a unified vision and clear objectives, their efforts were stalling. To right the ship, they brought in a Certified Coach, Chris Duprey, to facilitate their Alignment Day, help them align on their strategy, and set their Focus Areas for the next 90 days.

The impact was immediate. "We went from talking past each other to truly collaborating," Matt Patrick shared. "If we hadn't done that Alignment Day, we'd still be spinning our wheels. It was the catalyst we needed to get everyone on the same page." Since then, Patrick Accounting has seen dramatic improvements in communication, efficiency, and even their bottom line.

Alignment Day is just the start. Once your team is unified, the next step is to translate that energy and focus into a concrete plan of action. That's where the Endless Customers Quarterly Planning Session comes in.

> **Reader's Resources:** You can download a digital copy of the Game Plan, as well as other Quarterly Planning Session tools and resources in the EC Companion Guide.
>
>

Step #3: Hold Quarterly Planning Sessions

Coming out of the education portion of Alignment Day, your team will be all fired up and ready to hit the ground running. But with so much opportunity ahead, where do you begin?

To make meaningful progress on your journey to mastering Endless Customers, your efforts need to be focused. You can't tackle everything at once. Just like any other strategic business planning, the key is narrowing your focus to the most impactful initiatives.

That's where the **Quarterly Planning Session** comes in.

During this session, your leadership team will identify three to five top priorities, or what we call **Focus Areas,** for the next 90 days. These Focus Areas represent the most important work your team needs to accomplish to move the needle toward becoming the most known and most trusted brand in your market.

With the Focus Areas defined, your team will create a **Game Plan**—a clear roadmap that outlines the action steps required, assigns ownership to specific team members, and sets the timeline for execution. This process ensures accountability, clarity, and alignment across your organization.

Reader's Resources: Want to learn how a Certified Coach can facilitate your Alignment Day and guide your organization toward achieving Endless Customers? Contact IMPACT to connect with a coach and discover the right level of support for your business.

Endless Customers Planning Sessions and the work that follows operates on 90-day intervals. This cadence strikes the perfect balance: It gives your team enough time to make meaningful progress on your initiatives without letting things drag on or lose urgency. A quarter is manageable, motivating, and focused—ideal for driving sustained momentum.

At the end of each 90-day period, your team will revisit their progress, celebrate wins, and refine the next set of Focus Areas for the following 90 days. This iterative process keeps your team aligned, agile, and consistently moving forward on the path to Endless Customers.

Step #4: Repeat Alignment Day Annually

Alignment Day should be an annual event for your company. Teams evolve, new members join, and old habits can resurface. Revisiting the core principles keeps everyone aligned, speaking the same language, and focused on your long-term vision, ensuring the momentum you've built continues to grow.

While the principles may be the same things people have heard multiple times already, the business and even individual roles will likely have changed. So what they get out of an Alignment Day will be different every time. And let's be honest, it won't all stick the first time. As the saying goes, you have to hear something seven times before you really hear it.

In addition to your annual Alignment Day, you should offer regular coaching and training opportunities for your team to focus on continuous improvement.

And if a new team member joins between Alignment Days, your company should have a documented onboarding process in place to quickly bring them up to speed. This should include reading *Endless Customers* and understanding how their role contributes to the company's overall strategy.

26

Measuring and Tracking Your Success with Endless Customers

Alignment Day and Quarterly Planning Sessions give your team the clarity and focus needed to begin executing the Endless Customers strategy. But how do you ensure the work you're doing is effective? How do you track progress, identify gaps, and stay accountable to your goals over time?

That's where the **Endless Customers Scorecard** and **Typical Journey** come in. These tools work together to guide your progress, from your first Quarterly Planning Session and beyond. The Scorecard helps you evaluate your efforts and measure success, while the Typical Journey provides clear milestones to ensure you stay on track toward achieving Endless Customers. Together, they ensure your work remains focused, strategic, and impactful.

The Endless Customers Scorecard™

Just as Marcus relied on HubSpot's Website Grader to assess and optimize the performance of his website, the **Endless Customers Scorecard** is the primary tool businesses use to measure their growth and success with this framework. This tool is designed to help businesses assess their current position, set clear goals, prioritize efforts, and track progress over time. It gives you the visibility you need to succeed with the Endless Customers System.

The scorecard comprises 10 key prompts—two for each of the five components. These prompts are designed to help you identify strengths, uncover gaps, and create a clear roadmap for improvement.

To get the most out of this tool, it's important to approach it thoughtfully and consistently. Start by committing to completing the scorecard once a quarter as part of your Quarterly Planning Session. This regular cadence allows you to measure progress, adjust strategies, and keep your team aligned around the principles of Endless Customers.

Using this scorecard effectively requires honest and critical self-assessment. While the process is somewhat subjective, the key is to evaluate each statement carefully and score your organization as objectively as possible. The more honest and rigorous you are, the more value you'll gain from the exercise.

For the most accurate and actionable results, complete the scorecard as a team. Collaborative discussions foster shared insights, uncover blind spots, and ensure a more balanced evaluation.

Remember, this isn't about assessing individual performance. The scorecard is a tool to evaluate your company's overall execution and alignment with the Endless Customers System. It's a chance to identify opportunities for growth and build a stronger, more cohesive strategy.

If you'd like additional clarity or an outside perspective, consider working with an Endless Customers Certified Coach. Their experience with similar companies can bring objectivity to the process, helping you pinpoint where you stand and facilitating deeper insights that drive improvement.

For each statement in the scorecard, score your business on a scale of 0 to 10, with 0 being "We don't do this at all" and 10 being "We do this exceptionally well, 100% of the time."

Endless Customers Scorecard™

Organizations generally require 18 to 24 months to elevate their overall score to the 80-100 range. As challenging as it is for an organization to achieve a score over 80, it's just as challenging, if not more, to maintain it. But that's what the elite companies do. Rate each statement for your business on a scale of 0 to 10, where 0 is never true and 10 is always true.

The Right Culture of Performance

Our Entire Organization is Aligned Around and Trained on the Principles of Endless Customers

Leadership keeps this strategy top of mind for all staff, holds people accountable for their roles, and measures progress. Principles are regularly reinforced in company meetings and through company-wide trainings multiple times a year. All new customer-facing team members are effectively onboarded to our strategy.

_____ out of 10

We're Maximizing Our Growth and Improvement Efforts

100% of our team takes full advantage of learning opportunities, invests in their own growth, and is continually improving. Leadership has provided coaching and training opportunities to develop skills and avoid common mistakes. Our team consistently engages with and learns from other professionals growing with Endless Customers.

_____ out of 10

The Right Content

We're Consistent With our In-House Publication of Endless Customers Content

We've brought 100% of our content production in-house. We have someone on staff who's qualified, accountable, and empowered to oversee the success of our content strategy. We have produced at least one of each of the Big 5 for each product/service and are publishing at least three pieces of content per week, generally Big 5.

_____ out of 10

We're Leveraging Video Better than Anyone in Our Market

We've brought 100% of our video production in-house. We have someone on staff who's qualified, accountable, and empowered to oversee the success of our video strategy. We've produced and are using most of the Selling 7, publishing at least two Selling 7 or Big 5 videos per week. All of the sales team and SMEs are trained for on-camera performance.

_____ out of 10

The Right Website

We Have the Most Trusted and Best Performing Website in Our Market

When we evaluate our website against the competition through comprehensive analytics and adopting the perspective of our buyers, it's clear we lead the market. Our site excels in organization and clarity of messaging, bolstered by a robust learning center and efficient self-service tools, which together ensure a steady stream of sales-qualified leads.

_____ out of 10

We Manage, Update, and Optimize Our Website In-House

Our marketing team is proficient in handling most updates and changes to our website in-house and possesses robust skills in website optimization. They know how to expertly analyze website analytics, refine messaging, boost SEO, and enhance conversion rates — all without the need for external assistance, except for occasional design and development projects.

_____ out of 10

The Right Sales Activities

Our Sales Team is Fully Integrated, Aligned, and Supportive of Our Endless Customers Strategy

The majority of the sales team is consistently participating in the content creation process. The sales team knows how to find and use content effectively in their sales process, and is regularly doing so. Members of the sales team meet with members of the marketing team for a monthly revenue team to align on how both teams can best support each other.

_____ out of 10

Our Sales Team is Prepared, Trained, and Empowered to Close Deals Faster

We have a defined and effective sales process that's followed by the entire team, which includes using specific content and videos designed to help close deals faster. All sales team members actively participate in sales coaching, receiving feedback, and role-playing weekly, leading to better and more effective sales conversations, in-person or virtually.

_____ out of 10

The Right Technology

We're Optimally Using The CRM for Efficiency, Insights, and Better Customer Experiences

We manage all aspects of our CRM and sales/marketing technology in-house with limited needs for outside support. All members of the sales team and customer-facing roles are fully trained on the CRM and utilize it correctly and consistently. Leadership has the data, forecasts, and insights to make smart marketing and sales decisions to grow the business.

_____ out of 10

We're Using AI and Other Emerging Technology Better Than Any of Our Competitors

Our staff is proactive when it comes to researching, adopting, and experimenting with AI and emerging technology, staying ahead in a rapidly evolving digital landscape. We have clear expectations and safety guidelines for our staff to experiment with emerging technology, as well as a process that helps us measure the ROI of our experiments.

_____ out of 10

Your Total Score: _____ out of 100

What Your Score Means:

0-19: Our team is at the beginning of our Endless Customers Journey, and we will need significant overhaul and assistance to move forward on multiple key areas. (Est. 24-30 months to EC Mastery)

20-39: Our team is getting the hang of it, although we still require frequent assistance in several areas of our business (Est. 18-24 months to EC Mastery)

40-59: Our team is half way there! With occasional support, we can achieve success in several areas across our business (Est. 9-18 months to EC Mastery)

60-79: We have gained significant traction and our business is improving continuously, with very little assistance needed to achieve any given goal (Est. 3-6 months to EC Mastery)

80-100: We are able to do all processes with minimal assistance, and this is where most IMPACT Clients end up. (At EC Mastery, must be maintained)

The Right Content

1. **We're consistent with our in-house publication of endless customers content.** We've brought 100% of our content production in-house. We have someone on staff who's qualified, accountable, and empowered to oversee the success of our content strategy. We have produced at least one of each of The Big 5 for each product/ service and are publishing at least three pieces of content per week, the majority falling under The Big 5.

2. **We're leveraging video better than anyone in our market.** We've brought 100% of our video production in-house. We have someone on staff who's qualified, accountable, and empowered to oversee the success of our video strategy. We've produced and are using most of The Selling 7, publishing at least two videos from The Selling 7 or The Big 5 per week. All of the sales team and SMEs are trained for on-camera performance.

The Right Website

3. **We have the most trusted and best-performing website in our market.** When we evaluate our website against the competition through comprehensive analytics and adopting the perspective of our buyers, it's clear we lead the market. Our site excels in organization and clarity of messaging, bolstered by a robust learning center and efficient self-service tools, which together ensure a steady stream of sales-qualified leads.

4. **We manage, update, and optimize our website in-house.** Our marketing team is proficient in handling most updates and changes to our website in-house and possesses robust skills in website optimization. They know how to expertly analyze website analytics, refine messaging, boost SEO, and enhance conversion rates—all without the need for external assistance, except for occasional design and development projects.

The Right Sales Activities

5. **Our sales team is fully integrated, aligned, and supportive of our endless customers strategy.** The majority of the sales team is consistently participating in the content creation process. The sales team knows how to find and use content effectively in their

sales process, and is regularly doing so. Members of the sales team meet with members of the marketing team for a monthly revenue team to align on how both teams can best support each other.

6. **Our sales team is prepared, trained, and empowered to close deals faster.** We have a defined and effective sales process that's followed by the entire team, which includes using specific content and videos designed to help close deals faster. All sales team members actively participate in sales coaching, receiving feedback, and role-playing weekly, leading to better and more effective sales conversations, in-person or virtually.

The Right Technology

7. **We're optimally using the CRM for efficiency, insights, and better customer experiences.** We manage all aspects of our CRM and sales/marketing technology in-house with limited needs for outside support. All members of the sales team and customer-facing roles are fully trained on the CRM and utilize it correctly and consistently. Leadership has the data, forecasts, and insights to make smart marketing and sales decisions to grow the business.

8. **We're using AI and other emerging technology better than any of our competitors.** Our staff is proactive when it comes to researching, adopting, and experimenting with AI and emerging technology, staying ahead in a rapidly evolving digital landscape. We have clear expectations and safety guidelines for our staff to experiment with emerging technology, as well as a process that helps us measure the ROI of our experiments.

The Right Culture of Performance

9. **Our entire organization is aligned around and trained on the principles of endless customers.** Leadership keeps this strategy top of mind for all staff, holds people accountable for their roles, and measures progress. Principles are regularly reinforced in company meetings and through company-wide trainings multiple times a year. All new customer-facing team members are effectively onboarded to our strategy.

10. **We're maximizing our growth and improvement efforts.** 100% of our team takes full advantage of learning opportunities,

invests in their own growth, and is continually improving. Leadership has provided coaching and training opportunities to develop skills and avoid common mistakes. Our team consistently engages with and learns from other professionals growing with Endless Customers.

Total your scores from all 10 of the statements to get your overall score. Use this total to determine where your team stands on your Endless Customer Journey.

What Your Score Means

0–19: Our team is at the beginning of our Endless Customers Journey, and we will need significant overhaul and assistance to move forward on multiple key areas.

20–39: Our team is getting the hang of it, although we still require frequent assistance in several areas of our business.

40–59: Our team is halfway there! With occasional support, we can achieve success in several areas across our business.

60–79: We have gained significant traction and our business is improving continuously, with very little assistance needed to achieve any given goal.

80–100: We are able to do all processes with minimal assistance, and this is where most IMPACT Clients end up. Now, the focus is on maintaining this level.

It's perfectly normal to see a low score the first time you complete the Endless Customers Scorecard. Many businesses begin their Endless Customers journey with a score below 20, so if that's where you are, don't worry—it's expected.

As you work through the principles and strategies outlined in this book, your score will naturally improve. Over time, you'll see most areas rise significantly, but don't be surprised if some scores dip temporarily. That often happens as you gain a deeper understanding of what success really looks like and start scoring yourself more critically.

The beauty of this scorecard is its ability to pinpoint where you need to focus your efforts next. It's your roadmap for continuous improvement, showing you exactly where to double down for the biggest impact.

It takes most businesses 18–24 months to reach a score above 80, having successfully implemented the majority of what is taught in this book.

Now let's take a look at the Typical Journey most businesses go through on their way to achieving mastery of Endless Customers, along with the key milestones and scores you should strive to achieve along the way.

Reader's Resources: You can find a digital copy of the Endless Customers Scorecard tool, along with learning materials, resources, and examples, in the EC Companion Guide

The Endless Customers Typical Journey™

This roadmap serves as a guide for what most companies experience as they master the Endless Customers System over the course of 24 months. Every journey is unique—tailored to the needs, goals, and structure of your business. And while there's no one-size-fits-all playbook, there are core principles, best practices, and key milestones you should look to achieve along the way.

This timeline highlights the typical stages organizations experience as they implement Endless Customers. Milestones are tied to average scores from the Endless Customers Scorecard, which helps you benchmark your progress and refine your efforts. We'll explore how to use the scorecard later in this chapter.

The journey officially begins with Alignment Day, the foundational kickoff event discussed in the previous chapter. From there, progress unfolds through 90-day cycles, each building on the last to create sustainable growth.

The Endless Customers Journey™

This is the typical journey of a company mastering the Endless Customers System™ within 24 months. Use it as a guide to track your own progress, keeping in mind that each company's journey is unique. Some may advance more quickly, while others may need additional time. Along the way, businesses will focus on different elements, customizing their approach to meet specific goals and challenges.

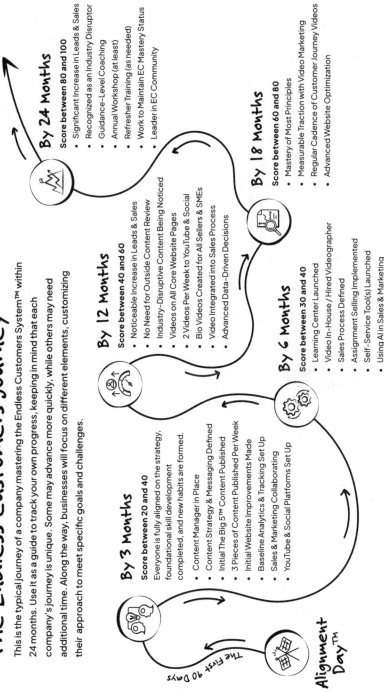

By 3 Months

Score between 20 and 40

Everyone is fully aligned on the strategy, foundational skill development completed, and new habits are formed.

- Content Manager in Place
- Content Strategy & Messaging Defined
- Initial The Big 5™ Content Published
- 3 Pieces of Content Published Per Week
- Initial Website Improvements Made
- Baseline Analytics & Tracking Set Up
- Sales & Marketing Collaborating
- YouTube & Social Platforms Set Up

By 6 Months

Score between 30 and 40

- Learning Center Launched
- Video In-House / Hired Videographer
- Sales Process Defined
- Assignment Selling Implemented
- Self-Service Tool(s) Launched
- Using AI in Sales & Marketing
- Paid Media Activated (for faster results)

By 12 Months

Score between 40 and 60

- Noticeable Increase in Leads & Sales
- No Need for Outside Content Review
- Industry-Disruptive Content Being Noticed
- Videos on All Core Website Pages
- 2 Videos Per Week to YouTube & Social
- Bio Videos Created for All Sellers & SMEs
- Video Integrated into Sales Process
- Advanced Data-Driven Decisions

By 18 Months

Score between 60 and 80

- Mastery of Most Principles
- Measurable Traction with Video Marketing
- Regular Cadence of Customer Journey Videos
- Advanced Website Optimization

By 24 Months

Score between 80 and 100

- Significant Increase in Leads & Sales
- Recognized as an Industry Disruptor
- Guidance-Level Coaching
- Annual Workshop (at least)
- Refresher Training (as needed)
- Work to Maintain EC Mastery Status
- Leader in EC Community

The First 90 Days

Alignment Day™

What Happens in the First 90 Days?

The first 90 days are about laying the groundwork for your Endless Customers program. This phase focuses on building the systems, strategies, and habits that will support long-term success.

During this time, businesses concentrate on putting the people, processes, and tools in place needed to get things started.

By 3 Months

- Put a content owner/manager in place.
- Define your content strategy and brand messaging.
- Publish your first content for The Big 5.
- Commit to publishing three pieces of content per week.
- Make initial website improvements.
- Set up baseline analytics and tracking.
- Launch into true sales and marketing collaboration.
- Set up your YouTube and social media platforms.

Endless Customers Score: Your score on the Endless Customers Scorecard is likely somewhere between 20 and 40.

By 6 Months

- Launch your Learning Center.
- Bring video in-house/hire a videographer.
- Define your sales processs and implement Assignment Selling.
- Launch your first self-service tool(s).
- Use AI in sales and marketing.
- Activate paid media (for faster results).

Endless Customers Score: By now, most companies have increased their score to anywhere from 30 to 40.

By 12 Months

- See a noticeable increase in leads and sales.
- No longer need outside content review.
- Industry-disruptive content is being noticed.
- Publish videos on all core website pages.
- Publish videos per week to YouTube and social.

- Bio Videos created for all sellers and SMEs.
- Video integrated into the sales process.
- Make advanced data-driven decisions.

Endless Customers Score: Typically ranges between 40 and 60.

By 18 Months
- Master most of the principles.
- Have measurable traction with video marketing.
- Establish regular cadence of Customer Journey Videos.
- Implement advanced website optimization.

Endless Customers Score: Anywhere from 60 to 80 and consistently climbing.

By 24 Months

If you and your team stay committed to the process and consistently implement everything in this book at the highest level, by the 24-month mark, you'll likely be the most known and trusted brand in your market. And that comes with major benefits—a healthy, sustainable business that's poised for growth, whatever that looks like for you.

By this point you should:

- See significant increases in leads and sales.
- Be recognized as an industry disruptor.
- Receive guidance-level coaching.
- Hold annual workshop (at least).
- Receive refresher training (as needed).
- Work to maintain EC mastery status.
- Be a leader in EC community.

Endless Customers Score: Anywhere from 80 to 100

Once you've reached the end of the Typical Journey, Endless Customers is now so deeply ingrained in your company's DNA that your only real enemy at this point is complacency. Why? Because when you stop innovating and pushing forward, that's when your competitors will catch up.

To prevent this, continue holding annual workshops, conduct refresher training as needed, and actively work to maintain your mastery status. The companies that remain industry disruptors are the ones that keep refining, innovating, and adapting. Endless Customers has brought you here, and by continuing to embrace its principles, you'll stay ahead of the curve for years to come.

Marcus will discuss the issue of complacency further in the conclusion, offering insights and inspiration to ensure you don't simply maintain your momentum but continue evolving as a leader in your industry.

27

Accelerating and Sustaining Your Success

Building an Endless Customers business is not a one-time task—it's an ongoing process of growth, refinement, and commitment.

The good news? You don't have to do it alone.

In our experience, we've found that there are two key factors that will help a business sustain and accelerate their success with Endless Customers. And those two factors are working with a Certified Coach who guides you through the process, and tapping into the power of the Endless Customers community.

The Importance of a Coach

Can you implement this system on your own? Absolutely. That's why the predecessor of this book, *They Ask, You Answer,* resonated with so many people and businesses—it's simple, straightforward, and rooted in common sense.

But if you want to accelerate your success, avoid unnecessary detours, and achieve remarkable results faster, the support of an Endless Customers Certified Coach can make all the difference.

Some businesses engage a coach right from the start, using them as a full-blown support system to help guide their teams toward mastery of the system. Others get started on their own or maybe bring in a coach just to facilitate key meetings, like Alignment Days and Quarterly Planning Sessions. There are also teams that don't require as much handholding and instead use a coach for these key sessions to ensure they're staying on track and not missing key opportunities.

Whether you're thinking about getting started with the Endless Customers System or you're already six or more months into your journey, it's never too late to bring in a coach to accelerate your results. Every business's journey is unique, and there's no one-size-fits-all approach to achieving success. The key is to assess what level of support will help you achieve the greatest impact.

Reader's Resources: Are you interested in learning more about how a Certified Coach can help your organization achieve Endless Customers? Reach out to IMPACT to speak with a coach and assess what level of support would be the right fit for your business.

The Power of Community

Being successful with Endless Customers doesn't just hinge on having a coach. The power of community plays a significant role in sustaining your success. The Endless Customers community is a vibrant ecosystem where businesses at every stage—whether just starting out or well-established—come together to learn, share, and grow.

When you join a community of businesses implementing these strategies, you unlock a powerful resource that can significantly accelerate your growth and success. Communities are behavior change-makers.

In this community, you'll find shared knowledge, experience, collaboration, and support that can provide you with the collective wisdom needed to navigate challenges and keep pushing forward.

Here are the key benefits of being part of the Endless Customers community:

- **Shared knowledge and experience:** Learn from others' successes and mistakes, apply proven practices, and save time by avoiding the need to "reinvent the wheel."
- **Collaboration and support:** Partner with peers, get feedback, and tap into a network that offers innovative solutions and vital support for your business challenges.
- **Comprehensive learning:** Access a wealth of resources—courses, certifications, and lessons—that help you master the Endless Customers System.
- **Engagement and events:** Join monthly video discussions and bi-annual conferences, connecting with others at all stages of their journey to learn, celebrate, and innovate together.

No matter how much you know or how hard you work, you can always benefit from the wisdom and support of others. The Endless Customers community is here to help you grow and sustain your success, long after the initial implementation phase. Joining the community is a strategic move that demonstrates your commitment to growth and excellence.

Reader's Resources: Want to join a community of like-minded business owners, marketers, and videographers? Check out the EC Companion Guide for a link to the Endless Customers community.

The Pride Cycle:
Why Giants Fall
Final Thoughts from Marcus

It always starts the same way.

You're sitting in your office, looking at another quarter of record profits. The business is humming. Your team is expanding. The market loves you.

And somewhere, in the back of your mind, a small voice whispers: *We can ease up a little now. We've made it.*

This moment—this exact thought—has killed more great companies than any competitor ever has.

I've spent the last fifteen years as a speaker watching businesses rise and fall, and I've noticed something fascinating: The companies most drawn to the principles of this book weren't the industry leaders or the high-flying startups. They were the ones in pain. The ones facing extinction. The ones who, like my swimming pool company in 2009, had hit rock-bottom and were desperate enough to try anything.

This is not a coincidence. It's part of an ancient pattern that has brought down empires, toppled industry titans, and humbled countless leaders. I call it **The Pride Cycle,** and once you understand it, you'll see it everywhere.

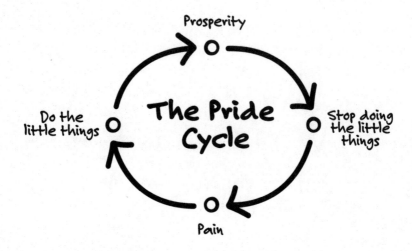

The Anatomy of a Fall

The cycle moves through four predictable stages:

1. **Pain:** This is where innovation is born. When your back is against the wall, suddenly all those "risky" ideas don't seem so risky anymore. This is where my company was in 2009, when we finally embraced radical transparency online because we had nothing left to lose.

2. **Growth:** As you implement these new approaches—these "little things" that your competitors dismiss—momentum builds. You start seeing results. The market responds. Revenue grows.

3. **Pride:** Success breeds confidence, but confidence unchecked becomes arrogance. You start believing you've figured it out and "pride" sets in. The hungry underdog becomes the comfortable leader.

4. **Complacency:** This is where the death spiral begins. You stop doing the little things that got you here. You dismiss new threats. Not only that, but you say things like "This is how we've always done it," or "If it's not broken, don't fix it."

Then the market shifts. A new competitor emerges. Technology evolves. And suddenly, you're back in pain—if you survive at all.

The Graveyard of Giants

Think about it: Why did Blockbuster laugh Netflix out of their boardroom? Why did Kodak, which invented the digital camera, stick to film until it was too late? Why did BlackBerry dismiss the iPhone as a toy?

It wasn't a lack of resources.

It wasn't a lack of talent.

It was The Pride Cycle.

These companies stopped doing the little things. They stopped innovating when they were successful. They forgot that the market never stops evolving, never stops demanding more, and never stops rewarding those willing to take risks.

Breaking the Cycle

Here's the beautiful truth. The Pride Cycle only has power if you're unaware of it. Once you recognize it, you can break it.

The key is to maintain your hunger even in abundance. To keep doing the little things—especially when you don't think you need to. To stay paranoid about complacency even when business is booming.

This means:

- Continuing to obsess over customer questions even when you're the market leader
- Maintaining radical transparency even when you have something to lose
- Embracing new platforms and technologies even when the old ones still work
- Questioning your assumptions especially when they seem most solid
- Constantly noticing opportunities for ways you can disrupt your industry—including your own business system
- Pushing the bounds of what it means to become a media company

Your Challenge

As we close this book, I want to leave you with a challenge: Look at your business right now.

Where are you in The Pride Cycle? Are you in pain, hungry for change? Are you in growth, seeing the rewards of innovation? Are you in pride, feeling untouchable? Or are you in complacency, resting on past successes?

Whatever your answer, commit today to **do the little things.** Not just this week, not just this quarter, but every single day. Commit to maintaining that hunger even when your company is feasting. Commit to questioning your assumptions even when they seem most solid.

Because here's what I know: The market doesn't care about our past successes. It doesn't care about our legacy. It only cares about what we're willing to do today, right now, to earn its trust.

The principles in this book—the commitment to transparency, to disruption, and to meeting your customers where they are—aren't just sales and marketing tactics. They're a mindset. A mindset that, if maintained, can break The Pride Cycle and build a business that truly lasts.

The choice is yours.

Will you wait for pain to force your innovation? Or will you choose to stay hungry, to keep doing the little things, to keep pushing forward—especially when it feels unnecessary?

But if you've made it this far in the book, I already know your answer.

And to that, I say, well done.

Keep going.

And never stop.

Seeking Your Help and How to Reach Out

If you enjoyed this book, I and the team at IMPACT would be incredibly grateful for a review on Amazon. I know this is a lot to ask, but it makes a massive difference in the success of the book, as well as the Endless Customers movement.

And if you have a question for me personally, just email me at Marcus@ EndlessCustomers.com.

Notes

Chapter 1

1. Redbord, Michael. "The Hard Truth About Acquisition Costs (and How Your Customers Can Save You)." *HubSpot* (blog), August 2, 2023. https://blog.hubspot.com/service/customer-acquisition-study.
2. Wizdo, Lori. "Myth Busting 101: Insights into the B2B Buyer Journey." Forrester, July 13, 2017. https://www.forrester.com/blogs/15-05-25-myth_busting_101_insights_intothe_b2b_buyer_journey/.

Chapter 3

1. Fishkin, Rand. "In 2020, Two Thirds of Google Searches Ended Without a Click." SparkToro, March 22, 2021. https://sparktoro.com/blog/in-2020-two-thirds-of-google-searches-ended-without-a-click/.
2. Patel, Neil, "Zero Click Searches & How They Impact SEO." https://neilpatel.com/blog/zero-click-searches/?amp.

Chapter 15

1. Sprout Social. "US Social Media Trends for 2022 & Beyond." *Sprout Social Index*, 2022. https://media.sproutsocial.com/uploads/The-Sprout-Social-Index-Edition-XVIII_US-Forecast.pdf.

Chapter 17

1. Gartner. "Global Software Trends and Buyer Behavior Insights 2022." Gartner, 2022. https://www.gartner.com/en/digital-markets/insights/2022-global-buyer-trends-ebook.

Chapter 21

1. HubSpot. "What Do 76% of Consumers Want From Your Website? [New Data]." HubSpot Blog (blog), July 28, 2017. https://blog.hubspot.com/blog/tabid/6307/bid/14953/what-do-76-of-consumers-want-from-your-website-new-data.aspx.

Acknowledgments

This book is more than just the story of myself and IMPACT—it's built on the wisdom, passion, and support of many who have helped bring *Endless Customers* to life.

To IMPACT clients and the Endless Customers community who have continued to push what it means to "think like a buyer," thank you for your trust and belief in us. This book is a product of our collaboration, and it wouldn't be possible without your stories and insights. It's an honor to learn from you and share your successes.

Special shoutout to the following teams for allowing us to share your success in this book: Yale Appliance, Sheffield Metals, RetroFoam of Michigan, Beyond the Office Door (BTOD.com), Opes Partners, Sportsman Boats, Bahler Brothers, AIS, Shasta Pools, CSI Accounting & Payroll, La-Z-Boy Southeast, Mazzella Companies, Neumann Monson Architects, Patrick Accounting, and AQUILA.

To the incredible IMPACT team, past and present—there are far too many of you to name individually, but please know how much we love and appreciate every one of you. Special thanks to Tom DiScipio, Vin Gaeta, Katie Coelho, Joe Rinaldi, Kaitlyn Petro, Christine Austin, and Melissa Smith for their dedication to this company for more than a decade through all the ups and downs.

A special shoutout to Dia Vavruska, Carolyn Edgecomb, and Stephanie Baiocchi—this book wouldn't exist without you. To Chris Duprey and Zach Basner for bringing these concepts to life, integrating them with

IMPACT's services, launching our coaching programs, and helping refine the ideas in this book. To Becca Manganello, Kristen Pecka, John Becker, Jessica Palmeri, Nicole Cimo-Holmon, Alex Winter, and Austin Mock— your contributions here are deeply appreciated.

To our manuscript readers—Darin "Doc" Berntson, Keven Ellison, Alex Foulke, Erin Fults, David Larson, Mark Massey, Ed McKnight, Mike Minissale, Kaitlyn Pintarich, Julianne Roth, and David Meerman Scott— thank you for your precious time and feedback; you are forever part of this book.

To my amazing wife, Nikki; my four children, Danielle, JT, Larsen, and Pink; my son-in-law, Tevita; my daughter-in-law, Victoria; and my grandson, Mana: Thank you for joining me on this incredible journey. You are my everything.

And finally, to my business partner, Bob Ruffolo, for continuing to bring the vision of *They Ask, You Answer* and now *Endless Customers* to life over these past seven years together. The second edition of *They Ask, You Answer* would never have been written without you—you were the one who wanted to go "all in" with our clients on this system (for which so many are grateful). And you were certainly the one who brought the idea of *Endless Customers* into existence as well. Your contributions can't be overstated. Thank you.

About the Author and IMPACT

Marcus Sheridan is a highly sought-after international keynote speaker, author, and business strategist who has transformed the way companies connect with their audiences. Hailed as one of the top marketing and sales speakers in the world, Marcus began his journey when he co-founded River Pools. During the 2008 recession, he pioneered strategies that not only saved the company but also revolutionized how businesses educate and empower their buyers. This philosophy became the foundation for *They Ask, You Answer*, which continues to inspire leaders globally.

Building on that success, Marcus also co-founded **The Question First Group** (www.questionfirstgroup.com), a sales and leadership coaching company that is reshaping the way business leaders communicate, ask questions, and build trust in-person with their audiences. In addition, he is the co-founder of **PriceGuide.Ai,** the internet's most effective Pricing Estimator tool, enabling businesses to quickly and cost-effectively create a pricing estimator for their products or services—ultimately attracting more leads than ever before.

Today, Marcus is also a partner at **IMPACT**, where he and the team help businesses implement the Endless Customers System to become the most known and trusted brands in their markets. By aligning leadership, coaching teams, and equipping marketing and sales departments with the tools and training they need, IMPACT helps companies capture the attention of their buyers, earn their trust, and close sales faster.

Through this model, companies learn to attract qualified leads and transform the customer experience, all while aligning their entire organization around one goal: to dominate their market. Beyond coaching, IMPACT provides supplemental services, including website design and development, HubSpot implementation, and paid media services—all designed to amplify your results.

For Additional Help and Information

Marcus and the IMPACT team are here to guide you step by step through implementing the Endless Customers System.

Here are three ways to get started:

1. **Book Marcus to Speak:** Looking to inspire your team or audience? Marcus delivers dynamic keynotes and workshops on the strategies from *Endless Customers* and *They Ask, You Answer*, and how to build trust in today's marketplace. To book Marcus to speak at your event, email him at Marcus@MarcusSheridan.com or visit his speaking website at www.MarcusSheridan.com.

2. **Coaching and Training:** Work directly with the Certified Coaches at IMPACT to guide your business through your Endless Customers implementation. Learn more at www.IMPACTPlus.com.

3. **Join the Community:** Become a member of IMPACT+ to access exclusive resources, on-demand training, and a community of like-minded business professionals. Plus, attend one of our in-person Endless Customers events to dive deeper into the methodology. Learn more at www.IMPACTPlus.com.

Index

Are You Ready to Achieve Endless Customers?

If you want to dominate your market, grow trust with your buyers, and drive consistent, measurable sales results, **IMPACT** can help.

We **coach and train organizations** to take full control of their marketing and sales efforts in-house—because we know that's how the best results are achieved.

Our proven system, Endless Customers, empowers businesses to:

→ Develop effective **sales and marketing programs**

→ **Train your teams** on the skills they need to succeed

→ **Build real trust** with your audience

→ Foster a culture of **innovation and lasting market leadership**

IMPACT can help you transform your business into one where buyers **seek you out with confidence**, your team **performs at its best**, and you **dominate your market** by consistently delivering **value, trust, and expertise.**

Contact IMPACT to Speak with a Coach